Visual Reference

Microsoft
Money 99

At a Glance

Microsoft Press

PUBLISHED BY
Microsoft Press
A Division of Microsoft Corporation
One Microsoft Way
Redmond, Washington 98052-6399

Library of Congress Cataloging-in-Publication Data
Nelson, Stephen L., 1959-
    Microsoft Money 99 At a Glance / Stephen L. Nelson.
       p. cm.
    Includes index.
    ISBN 1-57231-993-3
    1. Microsoft Money.   2. Finance, Personal--Computer programs.
    3. Investments--Computer programs.   I. Title.
    HG179.N426148   1998
    332.024'00285'5369--dc21

                                                                    98-29960
                                                                        CIP

Printed and bound in the United States of America.

    3 4 5 6 7 8 9   QEQE   3 2 1 0 9 8

Distributed in Canada by ITP Nelson, a division of Thomson Canada Limited.

A CIP catalogue record for this book is available from the British Library.

Microsoft Press books are available through booksellers and distributors worldwide. For further information about international editions, contact your local Microsoft Corporation office or contact Microsoft Press International directly at fax (425) 936-7329. Visit our Web site at mspress.microsoft.com.

For Stephen L. Nelson, Inc.
Writers: Kaarin Dolliver, Steve Nelson
Editor: Pat Coleman
Technical Editor: Jeff Adell

For Microsoft Press
Acquisitions Editor: Susanne Forderer
Project Editor: Jenny Moss Benson

Contents

*"How do I import
a Quicken file?"*

see page 9

Favorite Accounts

Account	Ending Balance
FNB Checking	$2,345.69
Home Mortgage	($146,747.12)
Woodgrove Bank Checking	$4,612.26

Add an account to
your Favorites list
see page 17

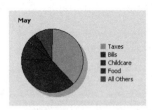

Learn about the types of reports and charts available in Money see page 55

"How can I use Money to plan for retirement and for other large expenses?"

see pages 70–71

"How do I download current stock market prices?"

see page 119

Monitor potential investments with Money
see page 121

7 Tracking Assets and Liabilities — 97

8 Investing in Stocks, Bonds, and Mutual Funds — 111

"How do I record depreciation and capital improvements on real estate investments?"

see pages 142–143

Add downloaded transactions to your account register
see page 155

Set up payroll subcategories
to track withholdings
see page 187

"How do I produce a balance sheet?"

see page 196

⑪ Managing a Small Business with Money   **171**

About This Book

Microsoft *Money 99 At a Glance* is for anyone who wants to exploit the power of Microsoft's personal finance manager, Money 99. You'll find this book to be a straightforward, easy-to-read reference tool. Based on the premise that it's tough to make "smart" decisions about money, this book's purpose is to help you use your computer as a tool to better organize and manage your financial affairs.

No Computerese!

Let's face it—when there's a task you don't know how to do but you need to get it done in a hurry, or when you're stuck in the middle of a task and can't figure out what to do next, there's nothing more frustrating than having to read page after page of technical background material. You want the information you need—nothing more, nothing less—and you want it now! *And* it should be easy to find and understand.

That's what this book is all about. It's written in plain English—no technical jargon and no computerese. There's no single task in the book that takes more than two pages. (And most take a page or less.) Just look up the task in the index or the table of contents, turn to the page, and there's the information, laid out step by step and accompanied by a graphic image or two to add visual clarity. You don't get bogged down by the whys and wherefores: just follow the steps, look at the illustrations, and get your work done with a minimum of hassle.

Occasionally you might have to turn to another page if the procedure you're working on has a "See Also" in the left column. That's because there's a lot of overlap among tasks, and I didn't want to keep repeating myself. I've also scattered some useful tips here and there and thrown in a "Try This" once in a while, but by and large I've tried to remain true to the heart and soul of the book, which is that the information you need should be available at a glance.

Useful Tasks...

Whether you use Money to track several investment portfolios or simply to help keep your checkbook, I've tried to pack this book with procedures for everything that you might want to do, from the simplest tasks to some of the more esoteric ones.

...And the Easiest Way to Do Them

Another thing I've tried to do in *Microsoft Money 99 At a Glance* is to find and document the easiest way to accomplish a task. Like most software programs, Money often provides a multitude of methods to accomplish a single end result, which can be daunting or delightful, depending on the way you like to work. If you tend to

stick with one favorite and familiar approach, the methods described in this book are the way to go. If you like trying out alternative techniques, go ahead! The intuitiveness of Money invites exploration, and you're likely to discover ways of doing things that you think are easier or that you like better than mine. If you do, that's great! It's exactly what the designers of Money had in mind when they provided so many alternatives.

A Quick Overview

This book isn't meant to be read in any particular order. It's designed so that you can jump in, get the information you need, and then close the book and keep it near your computer until the next time you need to know how to get something done. But that doesn't mean I scattered the information about with wild abandon. If you were to read the book from front to back, you'd find a logical progression from the simple tasks to the more complex ones. Here's a quick overview.

You'll probably turn first to Section 2. It introduces Money, explains how you can begin using Money, and describes some Money basics that you want to know as you begin exploring this useful tool.

If you're brand new to accounting software, you'll want to review Sections 3 and 4, which describe everything you need to know about using Money's account registers to keep track of your basic accounts. Section 3 describes how you use Money to keep track of your bank accounts, and Section 4 describes how you use Money to monitor credit card accounts.

Everyone should read Sections 5 and 6, which contain a wealth of information useful to all levels of Money users. Section 5 explains Money's Report and Chart feature. It talks in depth about the different kinds of reports and charts you can create, and why and when you would want to create some of the more common reports. Section 6 describes how you use the tools in Money 99 Financial Suite to build a budget, plan for the future, and track income and deductions for taxes.

Sections 7, 8, and 9 describe different types of specialized accounts you might want to create and use if you have loans, liabilities, investments, or assets you want Money to help you track. Section 7 describes how you can use Money to track your assets and liabilities. It goes through the different kinds of transactions you make in loan and liability accounts and provides several tips and strategies for getting out of debt. Sections 8 and 9 describe how you can use Money to track your investments. Section 8 deals with mutual funds, stocks, and bonds, and Section 9 deals with passive and active real estate investments.

If you have an Internet connection, you'll definitely want to review Section 10, which describes how you can use Money to bank online, make electronic payments, and browse the World Wide Web. This section discusses how to set up online banking and bill payment services with participating banks, and also discusses where you can find financial advice on the Internet.

The remaining section of this book delves into a more advanced topic. It discusses how you can use Money to keep track of small business finances. You'll only need to read this section if you have a small business and want to use Money to help with your business accounting. This section describes such things as invoicing, accounts receivable accounting, and preparing payroll.

Some Final Words

Let me close this introductory section with some final comments—comments, I hope, that you'll find helpful and encouraging as you use this book and learn Money:

Whatever you *want* to do, this book helps you get it done.

This book helps you discover how to do things you *didn't* know you wanted to do.

And, finally, this book helps you *enjoy* using Money.

I hope you'll have as much fun using *Microsoft Money 99 At a Glance* as I did writing it. The best way to learn is by *doing*, and that's what you'll get from this book.

Jump right in!

2

The Basics of Money

Getting started with Microsoft Money is really very easy because you don't need much prior computer knowledge to begin using the program That said, let me suggest that you'll benefit by having a little friendly help starting out and navigating your way through Money for the first time. This way, you'll get up and running more quickly, you'll quickly get the feel for Money's general organization, and you won't make simple mistakes that cause you to waste time later or miss out on some neat benefit.

Don't worry if you're not an expert on personal finance, budgeting, or investments. Of course, it helps if you know something about these topics, but this knowledge isn't required to make good use of Money. As a matter of fact, as you read through this book or flip to a certain page for help with a task, you are almost certain to find a financial tip or two or a definition of a term to help you out.

Getting Started with Money

To use Money, of course, you first need to install it. If you're not sure whether Money is installed, just click the Start button and then choose Programs. If you see Microsoft Money listed, the program is already installed. If you don't see Microsoft Money listed, follow the steps on this page to install Money 99.

> **TIP**
>
> *If the Installation Wizard for Microsoft Money 99 dialog box doesn't appear on your screen when you insert the Money CD in your CD-ROM drive, you can install Money the same way you install other Windows applications—using the Add/ Remove Programs tool in Control Panel.*

> **TIP**
>
> *Click Online Registration to register your copy of Money online. (You need to have a modem set up on your computer to do this.)*

Install Money

1 Insert the Money 99 CD in your CD-ROM drive. The Installation Wizard for Microsoft Money 99 dialog box automatically appears on your screen.

2 Click Next to start the Setup program.

3 Close any programs you have running and click Continue to continue with the setup.

4 Enter your name in the dialog box provided and click OK twice.

5 Write down the product identification number Money displays and click OK.

6 Click OK to install Money in the location it suggests.

7 Read the license agreement and click I Agree.

8 Click the large button beside the word *Continue* to begin installing the program.

9 When Money has completed copying files, click Restart Windows to restart your computer and complete the installation.

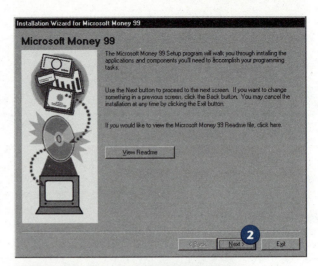

Installing Internet Explorer. *After you click Next in step 2, the Money Setup program searches your computer for Internet Explorer 4. Money 99 requires Internet Explorer 4. If the setup program detects that you don't have Internet Explorer 4 on your computer, it asks you to install it. Click Next to go through the Internet Explorer 4 setup program. After Internet Explorer has installed, click Next to start the Money 99 setup.*

If you're upgrading from a previous version of Money, Money 99 asks if you want to update your Money file to Money 99. You probably want to do this so that you can continue working with the data you've already entered in Money.

You can run the Personal Profile Wizard at any time by choosing the Tools menu's Personal Profile command.

You can install and run both Money 99 Basic and Money 99 Financial Suite in the same way.

Run Money

1. Click the Start button.

2. Choose Programs.

3. Choose the Microsoft Money command.

4. The first time you run Money 99, Money asks if you want to take a product tour to learn about the program features.

5. If you're not upgrading from a previous version of Money, Money prompts you to either create a new Money file or convert a Quicken file. Select Create A New Money File and click OK.

6. Money now displays the Personal Profile Wizard (called the Smart Start Wizard in the Standard Edition) to ask you a few questions about yourself and how you intend to use Money.

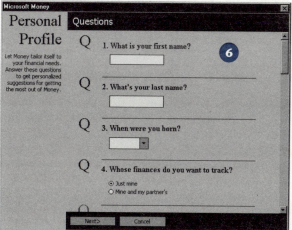

Creating and Opening Money Files

When you run Money, the first screen you'll see is the Home screen. At this point, you are ready to begin setting up accounts in the file that Money has created for you, or you can open an existing account, create another new account, or import an account from Quicken.

Open a Money File

1. Choose the File menu's Open command to display the Open dialog box.

2. Click the down arrow in the Look In drop-down list box, and locate the drive or folder in which your Money file is stored.

3. Double-click the Money file when you find it.

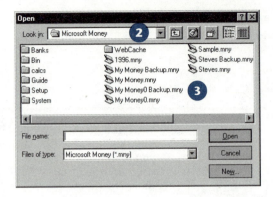

Create a Money File

1. Choose the File menu's New command to open the New dialog box.

2. Enter a name for the file in the File Name text box, and click OK.

3. Money creates the new file and displays the Personal Profile Wizard.

4. Use the Personal Profile Wizard to tell Money about yourself and the options you want in the file you're creating.

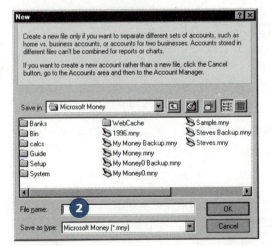

Import a File from Quicken

1 Choose the File menu's Convert Quicken File command to display the Convert Quicken File dialog box.

2 Click the down arrow in the Look In drop-down list box, and locate the drive and folder in which your Quicken file is stored. The default folder for your Quicken files is the Quickenw folder.

3 Double-click the Quicken file when you find it to start the Converter Wizard For Quicken, and click Next to continue.

4 Money suggests a name and storage location for the new Money file it will create from your Quicken file. You can change the name if you want, but keep the file stored wherever Money suggests and click Next to begin converting the files.

5 Click Finish.

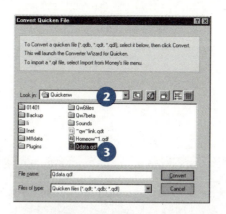

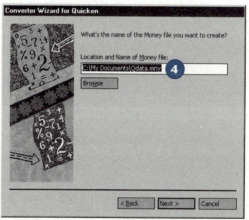

The Money Home Screen

Use the navigation bar at the top of every window to navigate your way through Money.

Click here to return to the Money Home screen.

Click here to personalize your Financial Home Page.

Click here to alternately display an account register or to view all your accounts in the Account Manager.

Money sets up a custom Financial Home Page for you after you complete the Personal Profile Wizard.

Click here to browse through articles on financial topics in Money 99 Financial Suite.

Click here to move backward through the windows you've recently visited.

Advisor FYI Alerts call your attention to low account balances, overbudget spending, upcoming tax and bill due dates, and other important bits of information. Money 99 Financial Suite's Advisor FYI looks at the transactions you've entered in your accounts and provides advice.

The Money Help pane lists the top five Help topics for the area you're viewing.

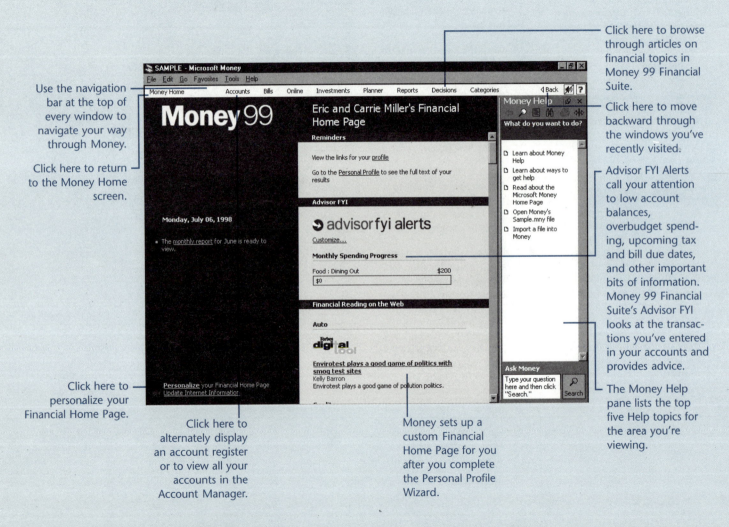

Getting Help in Money

If you have questions about how something works in Money, you can access Help in several ways.

Using the Help Pane

① If you don't see the Help pane on the right side of the Money window, choose the Help menu's Help Topics command.

② Use one of the following methods to get help:

◆ Click the Contents button to see Help's table of contents. To view information on a topic, click the topic heading hyperlink.

◆ Click the Keyword Search button to find a word or phrase in Help. Type a word or double-click a word in the list to display a list of Help topics including that word. To display the text of a topic, click its hyperlink in the list.

◆ Click the New Search button to display the top five Help topics for the area you're currently viewing. To learn more about a topic, click its hyperlink.

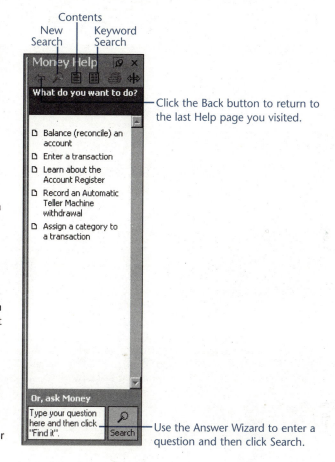

Contents

New Search

Keyword Search

Click the Back button to return to the last Help page you visited.

Use the Answer Wizard to enter a question and then click Search.

Archiving Money Files

Over time you will probably find that your accounts fill up quickly with dozens of transactions. After a year or so, you may want to rid your Money file of old transactions to make your accounts quicker and easier to work with. To do this, you create an archive file by removing selected transactions from selected accounts. By archiving your Money file, you still maintain old records; you just move them to another file to streamline your current Money file.

Archive a Money File

1 Choose the File menu's Archive command.

2 Enter the cut-off date before which you want specified transactions removed.

3 Click OK.

4 Enter a name for the archive file or accept the default name. Do not change the file type or the storage location that Money suggests.

5 Click OK.

6 Tell Money which types of files you want removed from each of your Money accounts by selecting options for each account and clicking OK to proceed to the next account.

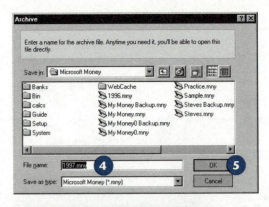

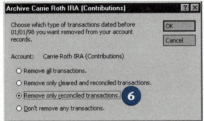

Backing Up Your Data

As soon as you start using Money, you'll want to begin backing up the financial information you collect. This ensures that you have a copy of your financial records in case the original is destroyed or corrupted.

TIP

You'll want to back up your Money files to floppy disks (or some other removable storage disks) in addition to on your hard disk drive. This assures that your files won't be lost if your hard disk drive fails or if your computer is stolen or damaged by fire or flood.

TIP

Money automatically saves as you work, so you don't need to save before you exit. However, you should still back up your files each time you finish using Money in case something happens to your computer and you can't retrieve your saved files.

Back Up a Money File

1. Choose the File menu's Back Up command to display the Backup dialog box.

2. Specify where you want to store the backup copy of your file:

   ◆ To back up your file to a floppy disk, click the Back Up To Floppy option button and select the floppy drive holding the disk on which you want place the backup file.

   ◆ To back up your file to a hard drive, select the Back Up To Hard Disk option button and click the Browse button to tell Money where you want to store the backup copy.

3. If you're backing up your Money file to your hard disk, use the Backup dialog box's Save In box to specify the disk and folder location for the file and click OK.

4. Click OK to back up the file to the location you specified.

5. If you have previously backed up to the same location, click OK when Money asks if it can overwrite the file.

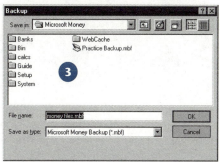

3

Keeping Your Checkbook

At its core, Microsoft Money is a computerized checkbook. Instead of keeping track of your checks and deposits in a paper register, you use an on-screen register. You get several important benefits from computerizing your checkbook records:

◆ Your computer calculates your account balances so that as long as you enter the correct numbers, your account balance is correct.

◆ You can describe checks as falling into specific income and expense categories. That way, you can find out how much you spend in a certain category with just a couple of mouse clicks.

◆ You can reconcile your account in roughly two minutes.

◆ You can print checks or transmit payments electronically, which makes paying bills much easier and much quicker.

Setting Up Bank Accounts

To use Money, you set up an account for each bank account you want to track. Then you open the register and record the checks you write and the deposits you make for each account. Money doesn't change the way you record checks and deposits; it simply provides an on-screen form for you to use in place of the paper register that the bank provides.

National Bank Checking

SEE ALSO

For information on setting up accounts for online services, see "Setting Up Online Services" on pages 152–153.

TIP

Money asks you whether you want to set up online services or create more accounts at the same bank only if you entered the name of your bank in step 2.

Create an Account

1. Click Accounts on the navigation bar once or twice to display the Account Manager, and then click the New Account button.

2. Enter the name of your bank or select it from the drop-down list, and click Next.

3. Select either Checking, Savings, or Bank from the list, and click Next.

4. Type a name for your account or accept the default Money provides, and click Next.

5. Enter the account number if you know it, and click Next.

6. Enter the ending balance from your last bank statement, and click Next.

7. If you don't want to set up any more accounts for the moment, click the I Have No Other Accounts At This Institution option button, and click Next.

8. Click Finish.

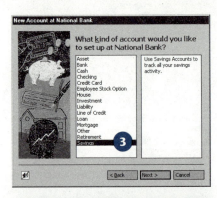

To open an account from the Account Manager, double-click the icon for that account.

Open an Account Register

1 Click Accounts on the navigation bar.

2 To move to the register of a different account, click the down arrow on the Accounts bar.

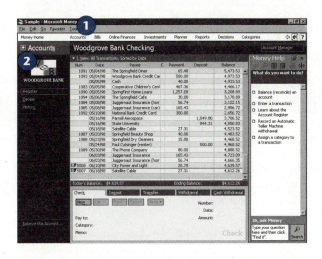

If you use an account frequently, it makes sense to check it as a favorite so that you can access it quickly. If you check an account as a favorite, it will appear on the Favorites menu and on the Money Home screen.

Add an Account to Your Favorites List

1 With the account's register displayed, click Details.

2 Check the Favorite Account box.

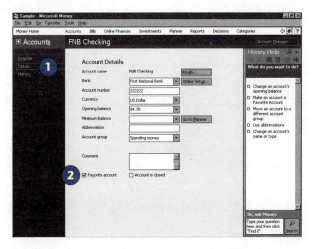

Storing Additional Account Information

You can easily store additional information about all the accounts you create. You can store notes about interest rates, minimum balance requirements, and transaction fees.

Go to **R**egister
Go to De**t**ails
Go to **H**istory

TIP

You can also use the Account Details window to edit the account setup. For example, you can edit the name of the account or the opening balance.

Store Information About Your Bank Account

1 Display the account register.

2 Click Details on the Accounts bar to display the Account Details window for the account.

3 Enter the minimum balance in the Minimum Balance field.

4 Select the account group that best corresponds to the way you use the account.

5 Use the Comment field to write notes to yourself, such as a reminder about fees you want to avoid.

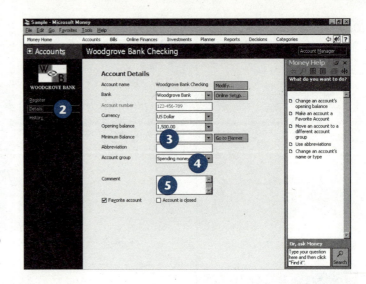

Recording Income

When you enter transactions in a register, you use the transaction forms at the bottom of the Account Register window. Click the tab you want to use, and then describe the deposit or withdrawal by filling in the fields. To move between the fields, press the Tab key or click the mouse on the field you want. When you finish, click the Enter button. Money records your transaction and recalculates the balance.

TIP

You don't need to record an income transaction for interest earned on your bank account. You can do this when you reconcile the account.

SEE ALSO

For more information about entering recurring deposits, see page 33.

SEE ALSO

For more information on splitting transactions between categories, see page 29.

Record a Deposit

1. In the bank account's register, click the Deposit tab, and if necessary, click New.

2. Optionally, enter a deposit number or check number in the Number field.

3. Enter the deposit date.

4. Enter the name of the person or business that is paying you.

5. Enter the amount of the deposit.

6. Click the down arrow in the Category field, and select an income category that describes the deposit.

7. Enter a memo for the deposit.

8. Click Enter.

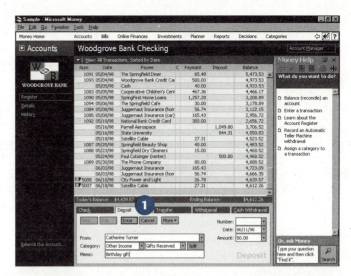

3

Using the Paycheck Wizard

As you well know, a certain amount of your paycheck is deducted right off the top of your earnings each and every time your employer pays you. Even though this money never actually makes it into your hands, Money can help you keep track of these deductions. Money can help you monitor how much you pay in federal, state, and local income taxes, how much you are paying for health insurance, and how much you put in employer 401(k) plans.

Record a Paycheck

1. In the bank account's register, click the Deposit tab, and if necessary, click New.

2. Enter the paycheck number in the Number field.

3. Enter the deposit date.

4. Enter the name of your employer in the From field.

5. Enter the word *Paycheck* in the Category field and press Tab to launch the Paycheck Wizard.

6. If Money asks if you want to track your taxes and deductions, click Yes and then click Next to continue.

7. If Money displays a series of dialog boxes asking if part of the paycheck is automatically deposited into a retirement or savings account, mark the appropriate options and specify into which accounts these deductions are deposited. Click Next to proceed through each box of the Wizard and then click Next to display the Paycheck dialog box.

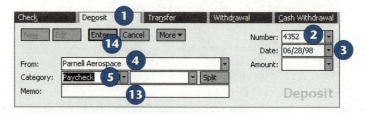

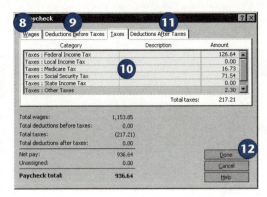

TIP

Employer retirement accounts. *If you have a tax-deferred retirement account through your employer, you can set up a Money account for it in the Paycheck Wizard by typing a name for the retirement account when Money asks. A retirement account works the same way as a regular investment account, so refer to Section 8 for more information about working with a retirement account.*

8 Enter your gross wages using the Wages tab of the Paycheck dialog box.

9 Use the Deductions Before Taxes tab to enter tax-deductible contributions to a retirement account.

10 Use the Taxes tab to specify how much you paid in income tax, Social Security, and Medicare.

11 Use the Deductions After Taxes tab to enter any post-tax contributions to a retirement account.

12 Click Done, and the Pay-check Wizard enters the paycheck amount in the Amount field.

13 Enter a note (such as the pay period or job) in the Memo field.

14 Click Enter to record the paycheck.

Category	Description	Amount
Taxes : Federal Income Tax		126.64
Taxes : Local Income Tax		0.00
Taxes : Medicare Tax		16.73
Taxes : Social Security Tax		71.54
Taxes : State Income Tax		0.00
Taxes : Other Taxes		2.30
	Total taxes:	217.21

Total wages:	1,153.85
Total deductions before taxes:	0.00
Total taxes:	(217.21)
Total deductions after taxes:	0.00
Net pay:	936.64
Unassigned:	0.00
Paycheck total:	**936.64**

3

Recording Expenses

Recording expenses works in much the same way as recording income. The only real difference is which tab of the bank account's transaction form you use.

SEE ALSO

If a check falls into more than one category, see "Splitting Transactions" on page 29.

TIP

If you can't find a category that adequately describes an income or expense, you can create a new category by entering it in the Category box. When you click Enter, Money displays a dialog box that asks you to name and describe the category. You can also create subcategories within categories in the same way.

Record a Check

1. In the bank account's register, click the Check tab, and if necessary, click New.

2. Enter the check number, or type *P* for Print.

3. Enter the check date.

4. Enter the name of the person or business you're paying.

5. Enter the check amount.

6. Click the down arrow in the Category field, and select an expense category that describes the check.

7. Click Enter to record the check.

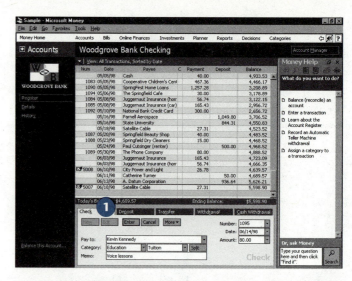

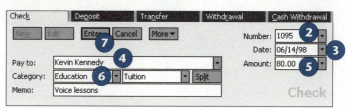

You can use either the Withdrawal tab or the Check tab to record debit card purchases.

Record an ATM Withdrawal

1 In the bank account's register, click the Cash Withdrawal tab, and if necessary, click New.

2 Enter the withdrawal date.

3 Enter the withdrawal amount.

4 Categorize the cash withdrawal using the Category fields or the Split button.

5 Enter a memo to describe the withdrawal.

6 Click Enter to record the withdrawal.

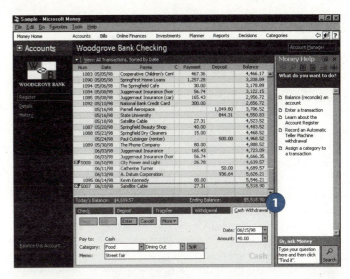

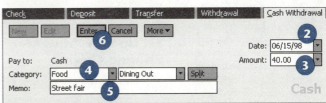

3

Printing Checks

You don't need to print your checks with Money, but many users do. The idea is that you save time—and produce neater check forms—by doing so. When you choose to print checks, Money uses the information that you enter when you record your checks.

TIP

Make sure that you describe all of the checks you want to print by specifying their Number as Print when you enter them in the register. If you forget to do this, you need to go back and edit the checks by entering Print in the Number field.

Describe a Check To Be Printed

1 When you enter a check in a register, type the letter P in the Number field. If you haven't recorded the payee's address in Money before, Money displays a dialog box asking for it.

2 If you're sending the check through the mail in a window envelope, enter the payee's address.

3 Click OK.

4 Click Enter to record the check.

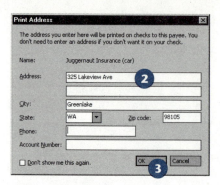

Set Up Your Printer for Printing Checks

1 Choose the File menu's Print Setup command and the Print Setup submenu's Check Setup command.

2 Select the printer on which you want to print the checks.

3 Select the type of check form you're using.

4 If you use a specific tray for loading check forms, select the printer tray in the Source field.

5 Click OK.

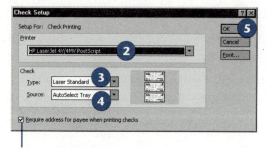

Unless you use window envelopes to send your checks, clear the Require Address For Payee When Printing Checks box. You don't always need to enter the payee's address when you print a check.

Print a Check

1. Display the checking account register.

2. Click Print Checks on the Accounts bar. (This button appears only after you've described a check you want to print.)

3. If you want to print only some checks, click the Selected Checks option button.

4. If you specify that you want to print only selected checks, Money displays the Select Checks dialog box. Click the checks you want to print, and then click OK to close the Select Checks dialog box.

5. Look at the preprinted number of your first check form, and enter this number in the Number of First Check in Printer field.

6. Load the appropriate number of checks in your printer, and click Print. Money prints your computer checks.

7. If the computer checks printed correctly, click Finish. If they didn't, click Reprint.

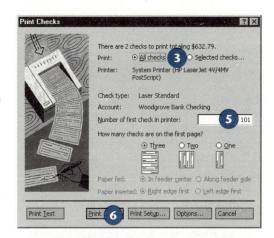

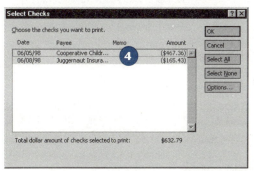

Entering Transactions in Other Currencies

If you withdraw money or make a purchase in another country, you can use Money's Currency Converter to convert the amount you spend into your local currency.

Use the Currency Converter

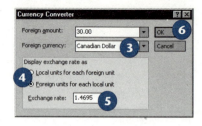

1. When you record the transaction, enter the amount you spent in the foreign currency in the Amount field.

2. While still in the Amount field, press the F8 key or choose the Tools menu's Currency Converter command to open the Currency Converter.

3. Select the foreign currency from which you want to convert.

4. Select an option for how you want to specify the exchange rate.

5. Enter the exchange rate for the day that the transaction took place.

6. Click OK. Money enters the corresponding amount of your local currency in the Amount field.

Timesaving Tips for Entering Transactions

◆ You can enter transactions directly in the register without using transaction forms (the tabs at the bottom of the Account Register window) by clicking the View down arrow and choosing Enter Transactions Directly Into The Register. Then click the View down arrow again, and choose All Transaction Details so that you can enter category and memo descriptions directly into the register as well.

◆ AutoComplete remembers every transaction you make, and if it thinks it recognizes a payee name as you're typing, it fills in the rest of the name for you so that you don't have to keep typing. If AutoComplete is correct, just press the Tab key to have it fill out the rest of the check for you. (You can change the check amount or any of the other fields if necessary.) If you don't want to accept the match AutoComplete finds, just continue typing.

Pay to:	Springfield Autobody

◆ If you want to enter a memo to yourself that you don't want to appear on a printed check or an online payment, just put the memo inside curly brackets ({}) in the Pay To field.

Pay to:	Sean Chai {Karin's teacher}

◆ To enter today's date in the Date field, type Ctrl+D. Type a plus sign (+) to go to the next day or a minus sign (-) to go to the previous day.

◆ AutoComplete by default enters the next check number if you tell it you want to record another check. Click the plus sign (+) to go to the following number or the minus sign (-) to go to the previous number.

◆ Click the down arrow in the Date field to enter a date using the Calendar. Click the arrows at the sides of the month to go forward or backward through the months to find a date; then click the date to enter it in the Date field.

◆ If you need to add, subtract, multiply, or divide numbers to get a deposit or withdrawal amount, click the down arrow beside the Amount field to display the Calculator. Click the numbers and operators, and then click = to calculate the amount.

Recording Transfers

There's a good chance that you have both a checking account and a savings account. If this is the case, you should know how to record one other type of bank account transaction, an account transfer. This works pretty much like you'd expect: you need to identify the accounts you're moving money between, the date of the transfer, and the amount of the transfer.

National Bank Checking   National Bank Credit Card

SEE ALSO

For more information about transferring money electronically with online banking, see "Transferring Money Online" on page 164.

Record a Transfer

1. Click the Transfer tab, and if necessary, click New.

2. Enter the name of the account you're moving money from.

3. Enter the transfer date.

4. Enter the name of the account you're moving money to.

5. Enter the transfer amount.

6. Leave the Pay To field empty.

7. Optionally, enter a note in the Memo field.

8. Click Enter to record the transfer and recalculate the balance for both accounts.

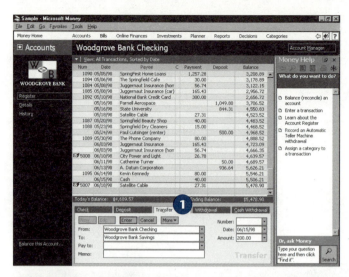

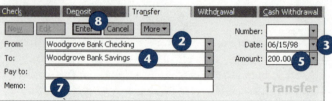

Splitting Transactions

Especially if you're a frequent "one-stop shopper," you'll often find that a single check you write falls into several categories. Fortunately, Money lets you split transactions into different categories. For example, maybe you wrote a check to a local grocery store, but the check didn't buy just one thing. You bought some groceries. You had a drug prescription filled. And you bought some flowers for a friend's birthday. Money makes it easy to record this check in three spending categories.

> **TIP**
>
> *You can add a new category or subcategory to the categories list by typing it in the Category or Subcategory box.*

Split a Transaction

1 Click the Split button. Money displays the Split Transaction dialog box.

2 Enter the first category on the first line.

3 Optionally, select a subcategory for that purchase or income.

4 Optionally, enter a memo to describe the first spending category. For example, you might want to list exactly what you bought.

5 Enter the amount spent or received in the first category in the Amount field.

6 Repeat steps 3 through 5 on the second and subsequent lines for each spending category and subcategory.

7 Click Done when you finish. Money closes the Split Transaction dialog box and returns you to the account register transaction form so that you can continue filling out your transaction.

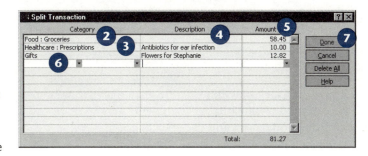

3

Working with Lists

You use the Categories and Payees area to work with your lists of categories and payees. Using these lists, you can add, delete, and move categories and payees. For example, if an individual or a company changes its name, you can change the name in the Payees list to reflect it. You can also merge payees if you find you have more than one spelling of the same name.

TIP

Select a category from the Categories list and click Modify to rename a category or to change it from an expense category to an income category (or vice versa).

Move a Category

1. Click Categories on the navigation bar.

2. Select the category or subcategory you want to move.

3. Click Move.

4. Enter the new category under which you want the previous category or subcategory to fall.

5. Click OK.

Delete a Category

1. Click Categories on the navigation bar.

2. Select the category or subcategory you do not need.

3. Click Delete.

4. Click OK when Money asks you to confirm the deletion. If you have existing transactions using this category, Money asks you to assign the transactions to another category.

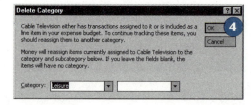

TIP

Click Go To Payee or Go To Category to display details about the selected payee or category.

Rename a Payee

1. Click Categories on the navigation bar.

2. Click Payees on the Categories bar.

3. Select the payee you want to rename.

4. Click Rename.

5. Enter a new name for the payee.

6. Click OK. If a payee already exists under the name you specify, Money asks if you want the transactions rolled into the existing payee name. Click Yes.

Entering Recurring Transactions

You can use Money's Payment Calendar to help keep track of recurring deposits, such as direct deposit paychecks, and recurring bills, such as monthly utility bills and automatic mortgage or insurance payments. Money's Payment Reminder reminds you when these bills are due.

TIP

When the recurring payment approaches.
When a payment is 10 days from being due, you will get a reminder in the Money Home screen. Go to the Bills area and confirm that you have enough money in your account to pay the bill by checking the New Balance After Entering column. Then check the boxes of the transactions you want to enter in your account register, and click Enter. Click Enter again to record the transactions.

Add a Recurring Payment

1. Click Bills on the navigation bar, and if necessary, click Pay Bills on the Bills & Deposits bar.

2. Click the New button.

3. Click the Bill option button, and click Next.

4. Click the More Than Once option button, select how often the bill comes due from the Frequency field, and then click Next.

5. Select the account from which you pay the bill.

6. Enter the date for the first payment.

7. Enter the name of the person or business you are paying.

8. Enter the amount of the payment.

9. Categorize the payment and click Next.

10. Select the payment method and click Next.

11. Specify whether the payment is a constant amount or whether it varies, and click Finish to add the payment to the Payment Calendar.

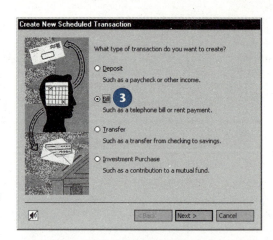

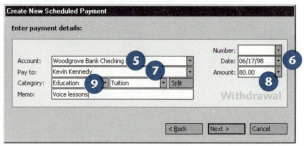

Add a Recurring Deposit

1 Click Bills on the navigation bar, and if necessary, click Pay Bills on the Bills & Deposits bar.

2 Click the New button.

3 Click the Deposit option button, and click Next.

4 Click the More Than Once option button, select how often the deposit is made from the Frequency field and click Next.

5 Select the account into which the deposit is made.

6 Enter the date for the first deposit.

7 Enter the name of the person or business paying you.

8 Enter the amount of the deposit.

9 Categorize the deposit and click Next.

10 Select a deposit method and click Next.

11 Specify whether the deposit amount is the same or whether it varies, and click Finish to add the deposit to the Payment Calendar.

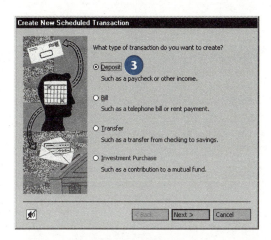

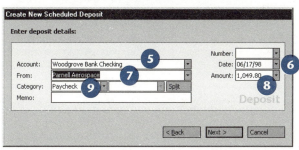

Paying Your Bills

You can use the Pay Bills tab of the Bills area to quickly record in your account registers the payment of scheduled bills, the receipt of scheduled deposits, the occurrence of scheduled transfers, and the scheduled purchase of investments.

Record a Scheduled Transaction

1 Click Bills on the navigation bar.

2 Select the scheduled transaction you want to record.

3 Click Record. (The name of this button changes depending on the type of transaction selected.)

4 Use the form Money displays to edit the transaction and add any additional information (such as the check number you used to pay the bill).

5 Click Record. Money records the transaction in your register.

Fixing Errors

It is easy to fix mistakes you happen to make while entering checks, deposits, and account transfers in your account register. Deleting or voiding a transaction is even simpler.

TIP

Money ignores voided checks when it calculates your account balance, and it doesn't include the checks in any reports. But it does keep a record of the voided checks, which is a very good idea.

Edit a Transaction

1. Go to the account register and double-click the transaction you want to edit.

2. Click the field you want to edit.

3. Enter your correction, and click Enter.

Delete a Transaction

1. Select the transaction you want to delete.

2. Choose the Edit menu's Delete command.

3. Confirm that you want to delete the transaction by clicking Yes.

Void a Check

1. Go to the account register.

2. Select the check you want to void.

3. Choose the Edit menu's Mark As command and the Mark As submenu's Void command.

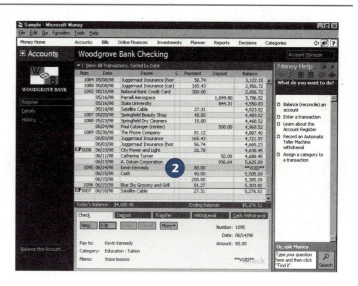

Finding Lost Transactions

Although Money can't help much in proving that you did indeed make that payment that got lost in the mail, it can give you a little peace of mind if you can't remember whether or when or how much you paid someone.

Search for Transactions

1. Choose the Tools menu's Find And Replace command.

2. Select which types of accounts you want to search.

3. Enter the text or number you want to find.

4. Select which transaction fields you want to search.

5. Click Next. Money displays a list of the transactions it finds.

6. To view a transaction, double-click it in the list.

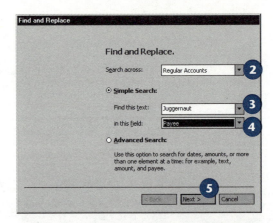

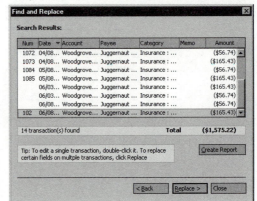

Replace Information in Transactions

1. Click Replace after Money displays the list of transactions it finds.

2. Select the information you want to replace.

3. Specify what you want to substitute for the information.

4. Tell Money whether you want it to replace the information in all the listed transactions or in only those that you designate.

5. If you choose to select the transactions individually, put a check mark beside the ones you want to replace.

6. Click Next.

7. Click Finish.

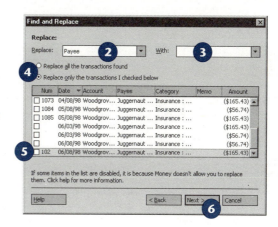

3

Reconciling Bank Accounts

Let's face it. One of the most tedious tasks in keeping a checking account is balancing, or *reconciling*, the account. Yet it's extremely important to do so. By comparing your records with the bank's, you can catch errors you've made in recording transactions and usually catch errors made by the bank as well. Only by regularly balancing an account can you protect yourself against problems such as forgery and embezzlement.

TIP

In Money's initial list of categories, there is a Bank Charges category for recording service charges.

Reconcile a Bank Account

1 Display the account register for the bank account you want to reconcile.

2 Click Balance This Account on the Accounts bar. Money displays an introductory Balance dialog box. Click Next.

3 In the next dialog box, enter the bank statement ending date in the Statement Date field.

4 Enter the bank statement opening, or starting, balance in the Starting Balance field.

5 Enter the bank statement closing, or ending, balance in the Ending Balance field.

6 If your bank statement shows a monthly service charge, use the Service Charge and Category fields to describe this expense.

7 If your bank statement shows any interest income, use the Interest Earned and Category fields to describe this income.

8 Click Next.

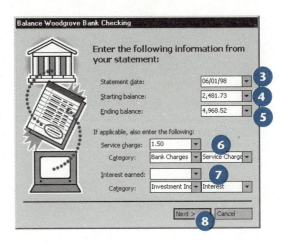

TIP

If you look closely at the account register after you've reconciled an account, you'll notice that Money changes the Cs you placed in the Cleared column to Rs. Those Rs mean that you've already used these checks and deposits in a reconciliation. Be careful, therefore, if you later edit these transactions.

TIP

If you want to force your account to reconcile when it doesn't, click the Automatically Adjust The Account Balance option button to tell Money to add a cleared transaction that makes the cleared balance equal to the statement balance.

9 Mark the checks and deposits that have cleared the bank.

◆ Click in the C (for cleared) column for all deposits that show on your bank statement. When you do, Money places Cs in this column to signal that these transactions have cleared the bank.

◆ Click in the C (for cleared) column for all checks and withdrawals that show on your bank statement. When you do, Money places Cs in this column to signal that these transactions have cleared the bank.

10 When the difference between the cleared balance and the bank statement balance equals zero, click Next. Money displays another dialog box congratulating you for balancing your account.

11 Click Finish. Money redisplays the account register in its usual format.

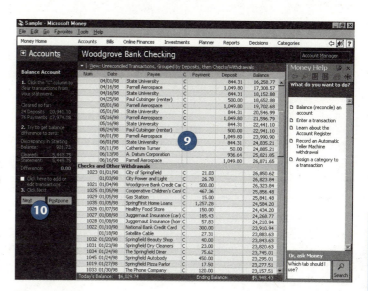

3

I Can't Get My Account to Balance

If, after you complete the step-by-step process described on the previous pages, the cleared balance still doesn't equal the statement balance, the problem probably lies in one of the following places:

◆ You made a mistake marking transactions as cleared.

◆ The register is missing one or more transactions.

◆ You or the bank recorded a transaction incorrectly.

If you find yourself in this situation, your best bet is first to be sure that your account register isn't missing a transaction. You can do this by checking that every transaction that appears on the bank statement also appears in the account register. I find, for example, that it's really easy to miss an automated teller machine (ATM) transaction or two. You can add a missing transaction directly in the Account Register window that shows when you're reconciling an account.

When you're sure that you've entered any missing transactions, verify that each transaction you recorded as "cleared" has really cleared. If you incorrectly marked an uncleared transaction as cleared, unmark it. If you accidentally left a cleared transaction marked as uncleared, by all means clear it.

Finally, compare the transaction amounts shown in your register with the transaction amounts shown on your bank statement. If you discover that you've entered one of your checks or deposits incorrectly, you can fix it by editing it in the list of unreconciled transactions. For example, you can change check or deposit information by clicking on the incorrect information and then editing or typing over the existing text or number.

Remember that in setting up your accounts, you need to begin with an accurate account balance, preferably a just-reconciled account balance. If you don't begin with an accurate balance, you might not be able to reconcile the account balance because your starting balance is wrong. In this case, there's not much you can do unless you want to go back to your old banking records and try to find the error or errors that made your starting account balance wrong. If you do find yourself in this situation, by the way, I suggest that you attempt to balance your bank account every month—and then give up once you can't go any further. (By clicking the Postpone button, Money saves your work and returns you to a regular view of the account register.)

This sounds lazy and perhaps crazy, but here's my logic. If you can't balance the account but the difference is the same every month—$41.35 in January, $41.35 in February, and $41.35 in March, for example—you'll know that the account won't balance because of errors you made at least as early as January. And in this case, I think it makes more sense to adjust the account balance so that your account does balance rather than waste any time looking for the error or errors that explain the mysterious $41.35. Money is, after all, supposed to make managing your finances less work, not more work.

To adjust the account balance, click Finish, even though Money still shows a difference between your records and the bank's. When Money displays the Balance Account dialog box, click the Automatically Adjust The Account Balance option button, use the Category boxes to categorize the adjustment, and click Next.

Two Notorious Bank Account Errors

Two types of bank account errors are notoriously difficult to catch, so let me tell you what they are and how you catch them.

♦ Transposing Numbers

For example, say you enter a check as $21.34 when it really should have been entered as $23.14. You've entered the correct digits, but in the wrong order. This error is tough to catch because as you look through your checks and deposits, you see the transaction, see that it has all the right digits, but fail to notice the transposed 1 and 3.

♦ Entering a Check as a Deposit or a Deposit as a Check

People make this error when they enter a transaction in the register but stick the amount in the wrong column. You can usually catch this error by marking your checks and other withdrawals as "cleared" in a batch and then marking your deposits as "cleared" in a batch.

Errors That Balancing Won't Catch

The main reason that you should balance bank accounts is to find errors you or the bank made in recording checks, deposits, and other transactions. But a reconciliation won't catch bookkeeping errors.

One such error is a transaction that you've forgotten to record in your account register and that hasn't yet cleared the bank. If the missing transaction is a check (and it most likely is a check, since you usually have more checks than deposits), you think you have more money in your checking account than you actually do. Unfortunately, the only way to avoid this error is to be diligent about recording your transactions.

Another type of error a reconciliation won't catch is a fictitious transaction you inadvertently recorded. Because the transaction is fictitious, it never shows up on a bank statement and is always listed as outstanding. Although the possibility of recording a fictitious transaction seems extreme, it can occur. You might, for example, record a weekly check to your daughter's piano teacher without actually printing the check.

Fictitious transactions have the opposite effect on your account balance than do uncleared transactions that you have forgotten to record: a fictitious check erroneously decreases the account balance, and a fictitious deposit erroneously increases the account balance. To prevent these errors, you simply need to be careful not to record transactions until they occur.

Closing Accounts

You probably don't close accounts very often, but if you do find yourself needing to close an account, you have two ways of telling Money that the account no longer exists. You can close the account so that you can still view its records and include its transactions in reports and charts, or you can delete the account and permanently remove all records of it.

National Bank Checking

TIP

A word of caution. *Deleting a Money account is a permanent action. If there are transactions in your account and Money asks you to confirm the deletion, the Money file is immediately deleted when you click Yes. You cannot recover it from the Recycle Bin. For this reason, you will want to be especially careful when you delete accounts.*

Close an Account

1. Click Accounts on the navigation bar once or twice to display the Account Manager window.

2. Right-click the account you want to close.

3. Choose the shortcut menu's Account Is Closed command.

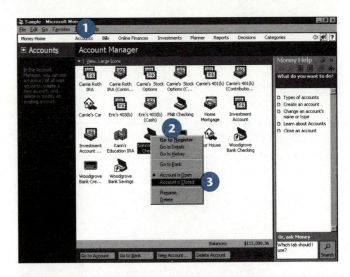

Delete an Account

1. Click Accounts on the navigation bar to display the Account Manager window.

2. Select the account you want to delete.

3. Click the Delete Account button.

4. If Money asks you to confirm the deletion, click Yes.

Keeping Track of Credit Cards

Almost every time I hear of someone in financial trouble, the person's credit cards seem to be one of the main culprits. Credit cards are by their very nature problematic. You're carrying around a little piece of plastic that can be used at whim to respond to the calls of sophisticated advertising. And once you've got that brand-new credit card and a high starting credit limit, there aren't really any obstacles to keep you from purchasing leather shoes you can't afford or expensive stereo gear you don't need. Then, after you fall behind and begin carrying a balance, breaking out of the credit card trap becomes more and more difficult.

Microsoft Money can help you deal with your credit cards by letting you track the money you're spending with a credit card and the balance you've accumulated. Keeping these records produces a couple of interesting benefits. The most obvious benefit is that you know where you're spending money and how much you owe on your credit card. There's also a more subtle benefit to using Money to track your credit card spending: if you're someone who finds it easy to spend freely with credit cards, the simple act of recording each and every credit card purchase will very likely help you become more sensitive to the effects of saying, "Charge it."

Creating Credit Card Accounts

If you're already disciplined about how you use your credit card, you don't really need to set up a credit card account. You can just record checks to the credit card company in the same way that you record any other check, splitting the transaction for each of the items you bought over the month. If, on the other hand, you do carry a balance on your credit card or you're not disciplined about your credit card spending, you should definitely set up a credit card account.

National Bank Credit Card

Set Up a Credit Card Account

1 In the Account Manager window, click the New Account button. Money starts the New Account Wizard.

2 Enter the name of the bank or financial institution that issued your card, and click Next.

3 Select Credit Card from the list, and click Next.

4 Enter a name for the account (or accept the default), and click Next.

5 If you know your account number, enter it and click Next.

6 The Wizard asks how much you owe on your credit card. Enter the amount listed in the Previous Balance portion of your current credit card statement, and click Next.

7 The Wizard asks whether the card is a credit card or a charge card. Select the appropriate option, and click Next.

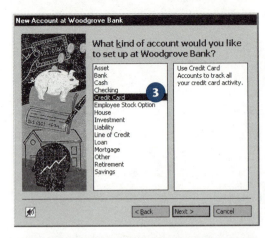

SEE ALSO

See pages 78-79 for information on how to use the Debt Reduction Planner to plan your way out of credit card debt.

TRY THIS

If you aren't carrying a balance from your previous credit card statement, you can save yourself a little time by entering your balance as zero. This way, you do not need to record the amount of your last payment.

8 If you selected the credit card option, the Wizard asks you about the card's interest rate. Enter the interest rate information, and click Next.

9 If your credit card has a credit limit, enter it in the field and then click Next.

10 Click the Keep Track Of Individual Credit Card Charges option button, and click Next.

11 The Wizard asks if you want the credit card payments added to the list of recurring payments. If you do, check Yes and fill out the dialog box. Click Next.

12 Click the I Have No Other Accounts At This Institution option button, and click Next.

13 Click Finish.

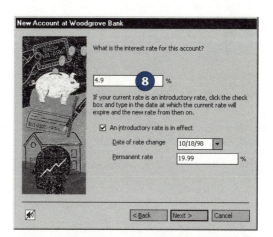

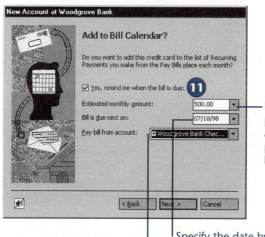

— Enter the payment amount you'll probably make here.

Specify the date by which you'll have to make your next payment on the credit card balance.

Indicate which bank account you'll use for writing the check that pays your credit card bill.

4

Recording Credit Card Purchases

To record a credit card purchase (or any other credit card transaction, for that matter), you display the account register of the credit card account. A credit card account register works the same way as a bank account register. To enter a credit card charge, you use the transaction form at the bottom of the Account Register window.

SEE ALSO

For more information about splitting transactions, see "Splitting Transactions" on page 29.

TIP

Don't worry about recording interest and service charges. You record these charges when you reconcile your credit card account.

Record a Credit Card Purchase

1. Display the register of the credit card account.

2. Click the Charge tab, and if necessary, click New.

3. Enter the purchase date.

4. Enter the name of the person or business you paid.

5. Enter the amount of the purchase.

6. Click the down arrows in the Category fields to categorize the purchase, or click Split to split the transaction into more than one category.

7. Enter a note in the Memo field.

8. Click Enter to record the transaction.

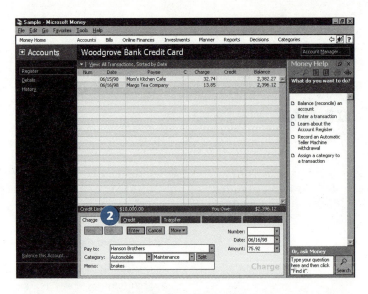

Recording Credit Card Credits

To record a credit card credit, such as you might receive when you return an item you bought with a credit card, you fill in the fields of the Credit tab the same way you fill in the fields of the Charge tab.

TIP

Although it might seem strange to do so, you want to record the credit using an expense category, namely the same one you used when you recorded the original purchase. This way, the balance in the category will reflect this refund.

Record a Credit Card Credit

1. Display the account register of the credit card account.

2. Click the Credit tab, and if necessary, click New.

3. Enter the credit date.

4. Enter the name of the person or business who refunded you.

5. Enter the amount of the credit.

6. Click the down arrows in the Category fields to categorize the credit.

7. Enter a note in the Memo field to help you remember why your account was credited: what exactly you returned or whether the business made a mistake when they charged your account.

8. Click Enter to record the transaction.

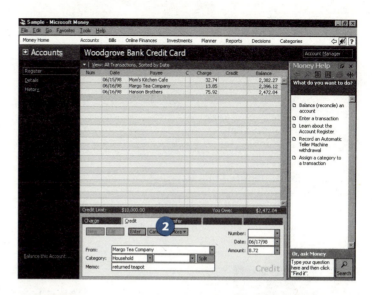

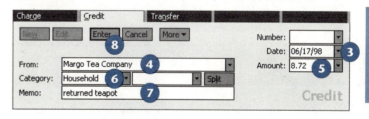

Reconciling Credit Card Accounts

Reconciling a credit card account works in exactly the same way as reconciling a bank account. Before you begin, you need your last credit card statement and preferably all your credit card receipts for the month.

Balanced on: 06/18/98.
Balance this Account...

Reconcile a Credit Card Account

1 Display the credit card account register.

2 Click Balance This Account on the Accounts bar.

3 If this is your first time balancing this account, click Next to continue.

4 Enter the credit card statement ending date in the Statement Date field.

5 Enter the previous balance from your credit card statement in the Total Amount You Owed Last Month field.

6 Enter the new balance from the credit card statement closing balance in the Total Amount You Owe This Month field.

7 If your credit card statement shows a service charge such as an annual fee, use the Service Charge and Category fields to describe this expense.

8 If your credit card statement shows any finance charges, use the Interest Charge and Category fields to describe this expense.

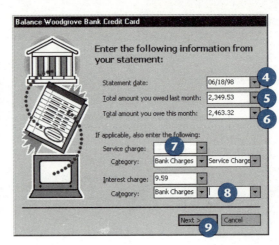

Balance Woodgrove Bank Credit Card

Enter the following information from your statement:

Statement date: 06/18/98 **4**

Total amount you owed last month: 2,349.53 **5**

Total amount you owe this month: 2,463.32 **6**

If applicable, also enter the following:

Service charge: **7**

Category: Bank Charges | Service Charge

Interest charge: 9.59

Category: Bank Charges | **8**

Next > **9** | Cancel

9. After you've completed the Balance Credit Card dialog box, click Next.

10. Mark the purchases, credits, and payments that have cleared the account by clicking in the C (for cleared) column. When you do, Money places Cs in this column to signal that these transactions have cleared the bank.

11. When the difference between the cleared balance and the credit card statement balance equals zero, click Next.

12. Click Finish.

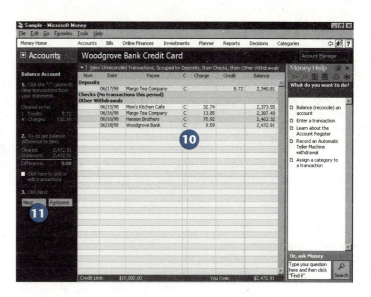

Recording Credit Card Payments

To record a credit card payment, you record the check that you use to pay the credit card bill in the appropriate bank account register. For example, if I am going to pay my credit card bill by writing a check on a bank account that I named "Woodgrove Bank Checking," I just write and record the check in the usual way. Then, rather than categorize the check, I transfer the money to the credit card account.

TIP
As with any transfer transaction in Money, you can record a credit card payment either in the register of the account receiving the money (in this case the credit card account) or in the register of the account giving the money (in this case the bank account).

Record a Credit Card Payment

1. Open either the credit card register or the register for the bank account you'll use to pay the credit card bill.

2. Click the Transfer tab, and if necessary, click New.

3. Enter the check number.

4. Select the name of the bank account you're writing a check on.

5. Enter the transfer date.

6. Select the name of the credit card account you're paying.

7. Enter the amount of the credit card bill you're paying.

8. Enter the name of the credit card company.

9. Click Enter. Money records the credit card payment and recalculates the account balance for both accounts.

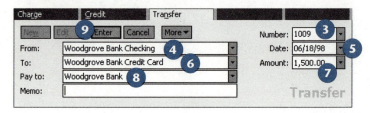

Using the Debt Consolidation Calculator

Section 6, "Personal Financial Planning," briefly describes the calculators in the Decisions area of Money. But because so many people have problems with credit card debt, this page elaborates on one of the calculators, the Debt Consolidation Calculator.

TIP

A word of caution.
Although it principally always makes sense to consolidate credit card debt into a tax-deductible home equity loan or into a low-interest personal loan, in practice, it often just gets people into more credit trouble. If you can imagine yourself spending more money and building more debt by having reduced monthly loan payments, you're probably better off being tough on yourself and paying off your credit cards the hard way, starting with the credit card that charges the highest interest rate.

Consolidate Your Debt

1. Click Decisions on the navigation bar.

2. Click Tools on the Decisions bar.

3. Click Debt Consolidation Calculator in the Calculators area.

4. Specify whether you want to build a consolidation plan based on the monthly payments you can afford or on the date by which you want to be out of debt. Click Next to continue.

5. Enter the balance, interest rate, fee, and minimum monthly payment amount for each of your credit cards. Click Next.

6. Enter information about any other loans you have and click Next.

7. Specify whether you would like to consolidate your loans into a home equity or personal loan. Click Next.

8. Review the results that the Debt Consolidation Calculator displays and click Next.

9. Click the Print button on the Summary tab to print a copy of your debt plan.

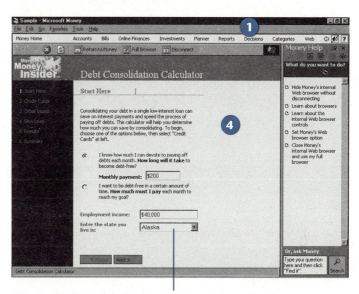

Enter your gross income and select the state you live in.

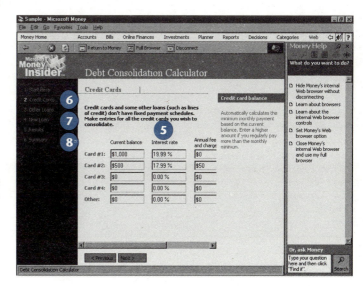

Creating Reports and Charts

Using Microsoft Money only for financial record-keeping delivers some benefits. Money, for example, calculates account balances automatically and accurately. It prints checks for you. And after you begin using Money, you'll discover that reconciling a bank account takes only a couple of minutes.

But the biggest benefit of using Money isn't that it allows you to do all these things. The biggest benefit is that Money lets you sort and summarize the financial information you collect in many ways. By using Money's reports, for example, you can see how much you're really spending on housing, groceries, work expenses, and so forth. You can easily track and tally tax deductions. And you can compare your actual income and expenses with whatever amounts you budgeted.

You can work with reports in several ways using Money. You can produce on-screen reports and customize them to show exactly what you want to see. You can also save your favorite reports to see how your spending habits change, and you can print and export reports to easily take them with you and show them to others.

Producing Reports

The makers of Money realized the importance of being able to visualize your finances, which is why they made the reports feature so quick and easy to use. Within a matter of minutes, you can create a detailed report of some aspect of your finances and customize it to show exactly what you want.

Report & Chart Gallery

TIP

To return to the Gallery Of Reports And Charts after creating a report, click the Report & Chart Gallery button in the upper-right corner of your screen.

Produce an On-Screen Report

1. Click Reports on the navigation bar.

2. Click a category on the Reports & Charts bar to see a list of reports and charts that summarize a particular aspect of your finances.

3. Select a specific report or chart from the list.

4. Click the Go To Report/Chart button. Money produces the selected report or chart.

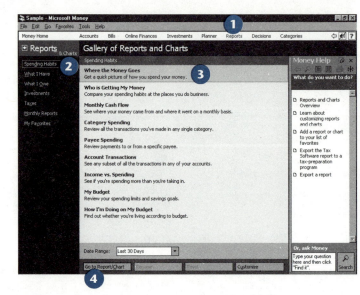

The Six Basic
Report Categories

CATEGORY	DESCRIPTION	PURPOSE
Spending Habits	Summarizes transactions by payee or category and compares actual income and spending with budgeted income and spending	Allows you to see how you earn and spend your money, where you earn and spend your money, and how your actual earnings and expenditures compare to your plans
What I Have	Summarizes account balances at a point in time or over a period of time	Allows you to estimate your net worth and to see the estimated value of your assets and liabilities
What I Owe	Summarizes liability account balances and post-dated payment transactions	Allows you to gauge the magnitude of your debts and to plan repayment strategies
Investments	Summarizes investment account and transaction information	Allows you to assess the profitability of your investments and to perform year-end investment tax planning
Taxes	Summarizes tax-related transactions	Shows you what taxable income and tax deductions you'll report on your year-end tax return and allows you to perform year-end tax planning
Monthly Reports (Money 99 Financial Suite only)	Summarizes your spending habits, investment performance, budget, debt plan status, and Advisor FYI tips for the month	Allows you to view several aspects of your financial situation during any given month and compare the information with other months

5

Working with Reports

After you create a report, you might want to turn that report into a chart so that you can easily see the information. With the click of a button, you can create a chart from a report and then customize the chart to your liking. When you have your report or chart just the way you want it, you can save it so that you don't have to re-create it the next time.

TIP

You probably want to keep the Show In 3D check box clear because three-dimensional charts frequently distort data.

Create a Chart

1 Display or create the report from which you want to make a chart.

2 Click a Chart button.

3 Click Customize.

4 Use the Customize Report dialog box to customize the chart.

◆ Click Bar to create a bar chart; then use the Stacked check box to tell Money whether you want your bars displayed side by side or in a single column.

◆ Click Line to create a line chart.

◆ Click Pie; then use the Pie Labels option buttons to tell Money how to label the pie chart.

5 Click Apply to preview the chart.

6 Click OK to return to the Chart window.

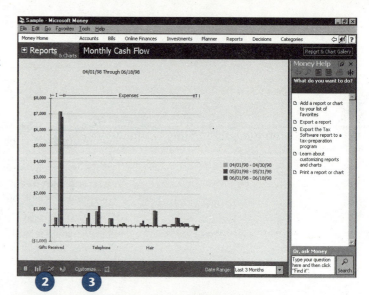

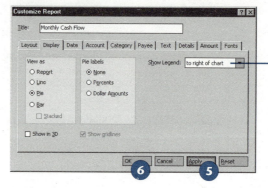

Use this field to specify where you want to display a legend.

Add a Report or Chart to the My Favorites List

1 Display or create the report or chart you want to add to your My Favorites list.

2 Choose the Favorites menu's Add To Favorites command.

3 In the Add To Favorites dialog box, enter a name for your customized report in the Report Name text box.

4 Click OK.

Producing Month-End and Year-End Reports

Money is capable of producing many different reports and charts. As a result, deciding which reports to produce can be a bit overwhelming. Fortunately, you can apply some good rules of thumb in this area. You should print out an Account Transactions report at the end of every month and file it with your bank statement and canceled checks. And you should print a Tax-Related Transaction report at the end of each year and store it with a copy of your tax return.

TIP
If you forget to back up your Money data, you can re-enter all the transactions from your Account Transactions reports to rebuild your financial records.

Create an Account Transactions Report

1 Click Spending Habits on the Reports & Charts bar.

2 Select Account Transactions from the Spending Habits list.

3 Click the down arrow in the Accounts field, and select an account from the list.

4 Click the down arrow in the Date Range field, and select Previous Month from the list.

5 Click the Go To Report/Chart button.

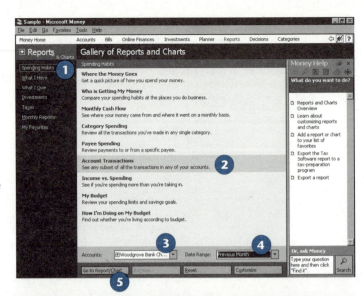

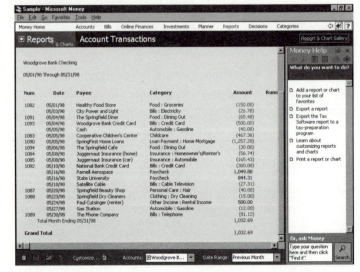

SEE ALSO

Section 6, "Personal Financial Planning," describes in detail how Money 99 Financial Suite makes it easier to plan your income taxes and prepare your income tax returns.

TIP

To create a Tax-Related Transactions report to export to a tax preparation program, click Taxes on the Reports & Charts bar, and then select Tax Software Report from the Taxes list.

Create a Tax-Related Transactions Report

1 Click Taxes on the Reports & Charts bar.

2 Select Tax-Related Transactions from the Taxes list.

3 Click the down arrow in the Date Range field, and select Previous Year from the list.

4 Click the Go To Report/Chart button.

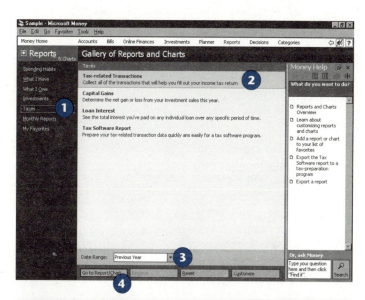

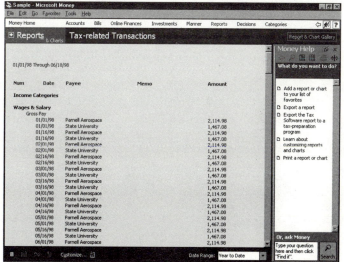

Customizing Reports and Charts

Since Money offers more than two dozen reports and charts, you can usually find one that answers the questions you have. Nonetheless, Money gives you a rich set of customization options that you can use to change the appearance of reports and charts.

Change the Layout of a Chart

1️⃣ Display the report or chart or select it in the Gallery Of Reports And Charts.

2️⃣ Click Customize.

3️⃣ Click the Layout tab.

4️⃣ Use the Layout tab's boxes and buttons to specify several layout options, including:

◆ What you want the rows and columns of the report to list

◆ How you want subtotals calculated

◆ How you want transactions sorted

◆ Which transaction fields you want included in the report

◆ Whether you want the chart to show a running balance

◆ What level of detail you want the report to show

5️⃣ Click OK.

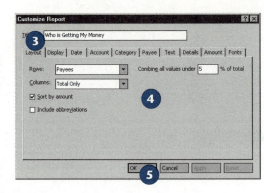

TIP

Which tabs and available options appear in the Customize Report dialog box depends on the report. Different reports have different customization options.

Filter the Information Included in a Report or Chart

1 Display the report or chart or select it in the Gallery Of Reports And Charts.

2 Use the field or fields available at the bottom of the window to customize the most common options.

3 Click Customize.

4 Use the Customize Report dialog box's Date, Account, Category, Payee, Text, Details, and Amount tabs to filter the information you want included in the report or chart.

5 If you're currently viewing the report or chart, click Apply to see your changes.

6 Click OK to close the Customize Report dialog box and display the report or chart.

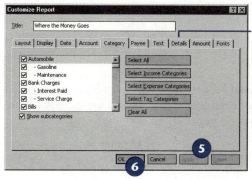

Use this tab to specify the type, status, or check or transaction number of transactions you want included in the report or chart.

TIP

The Reset button is only available if you've customized the report or chart.

Reset a Report or Chart to the Default Settings

1 Select the report or chart you customized from the Gallery of Reports and Charts.

2 Click Reset.

3 Click Yes.

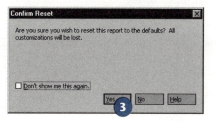

5

Formatting Reports

Once you have your report created and customized to show the information you want, you can also format it so that it is pleasing to the eye and easy to read.

Change the Column Widths

1 Select or display the report.

2 Click Customize to display the Customize Report dialog box.

3 Click the Fonts tab.

4 Select one of the Report Column Widths options.

5 Click OK.

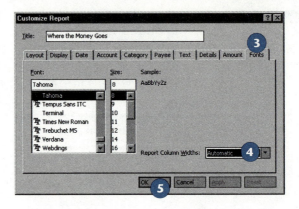

TIP

To undo all customization and formatting changes, click the Reset button.

TIP

Remember, you can't hurt your data by summarizing it in reports or by depicting it in charts, so feel free to experiment with customizing your reports.

Change the Font Style and Point Size

1 Select or display the report.

2 Click Customize to display the Customize Report dialog box.

3 Click the Fonts tab.

4 Select a font from the Font list box.

5 Select a font size from the Size list box.

6 Click OK.

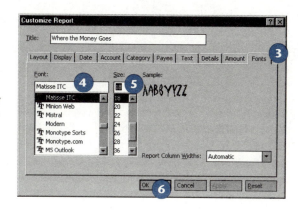

Printing Reports

Although on-screen reports are great, especially because you can create and manipulate them so quickly and easily, you may also want printed copies of your reports so that you can take them with you and show them to others—to your accountant, for instance.

Set Up Your Printer

1. Choose the File menu's Print Setup command.

2. Choose the Print Setup submenu's Report And Chart Setup command to display the Report And Chart Setup dialog box.

3. Select an Orientation option to specify whether Money should print pages in portrait or landscape orientation.

4. Click the Options button to display the printer's Properties dialog box, which you can use to change the paper tray, the print quality, and so forth. Click OK to return to the Report And Chart Setup dialog box.

5. Click OK.

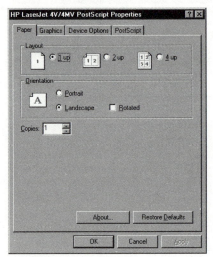

Print a Report

1 Display the report you want to print.

2 Choose the File menu's Print command to display the Print Report dialog box.

3 Select Print Range options to specify which part of your report you want to print.

4 Specify the number of copies to print in the Copies text box.

5 Click OK to print the report.

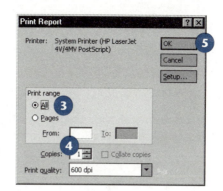

How Long to Keep Records

People throw around many different rules for retaining canceled checks, bank statements, copies of old tax returns, and other financial records. I suggest that you keep everything for seven years after you file a tax return. If you filed 1991's tax return in April 1992, keep all your 1991 tax return records until April 1999.

The reason you should hang on to your records for so long is that the Internal Revenue Service can examine returns as old as seven years. The IRS can't go back any further than that, except in a handful of very special cases. So as long as you keep everything together for at least seven years, you'll almost certainly be okay. (The "handful of very special cases" have to do with businesses with net operating loss carry-forwards and taxpayers with foreign tax credits. If you don't know what these are, they probably don't apply to you. But consult a tax advisor if you're not sure.) If you are ever audited, you can use Money to print a summary of your deductions, and you can verify this report with the canceled checks.

You should save some documents for much longer than seven years. When I say to retain records for seven years, I'm referring only to financial records. Hang on to insurance records permanently, for example, because it's possible in some circumstances to file a claim against a policy from years and years ago. You should also permanently retain many legal documents. (Consult an attorney for information on this.)

Exporting Reports

Exporting means to move a report to another application. You export reports so that you can manipulate the data in some way or use the data in another document. For example, you might export a report so that you can analyze it in a spreadsheet application such as Microsoft Excel. Or you might want to include a report in a word processing document.

TIP

When you export a report, Money creates something called a tab-delimited text file. *Tab-delimited text files are easy for spreadsheet applications to import and open, and they can also be imported and opened by most word processing applications.*

TIP

To import the tab-delimited text file in another application, just open it from the other application. (You may need to indicate that the exported file uses the .txt *extension.)*

Export a Report

1. Display the report you want to export.

2. Right-click the report and choose the shortcut menu's Export command.

3. Click the down arrow in the Save In field, and specify where Money should save the exported report.

4. Enter a filename in the File Name text box.

5. Click OK.

Personal Financial Planning

Personal financial planning might sound sophisticated, but it's really not. When you boil it down, personal financial planning covers three common-sense activities:

◆ Arranging your day-to-day financial affairs so you can spend more time enjoying life rather than worrying about how you're going to pay the bills

◆ Choosing and then plotting a course toward major, long-term financial goals, such as buying a house, sending the kids to college, or retiring

◆ Creating a financial safety net so that a personal tragedy or unexpected expense doesn't mean financial disaster

Fortunately, Microsoft Money 99 Financial Suite, which is the deluxe version of the Money software product, provides the Planner and Decisions Center tools to successfully address just these planning issues. This section describes these tools.

Using the Lifetime Planner

Perhaps the most powerful and useful personal financial planning feature available within Money is the Lifetime Planner. The Lifetime Planner allows you to construct a detailed, written financial plan that summarizes your current financial condition—and plots a path to future financial success.

TIP

Leave the life expectancy set to at least 90, even if this seems a little high.

Run the Lifetime Planner

1. Click Planner on the navigation bar.

2. Click the Lifetime Planner hyperlink.

3. Click the Welcome tab to display an introductory window that describes the Lifetime Planner.

4. Click the Next button to begin construction of your personal financial plan.

5. Follow the on-screen instructions when prompted by Money. For example, when Money displays the About You window, enter your name, birth date, and the age at which you plan to retire. If appropriate, enter your spouse's name, birth date and the age at which he or she plans to retire. Then add any dependents you have or plan to have in the future.

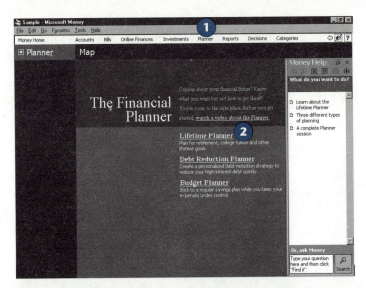

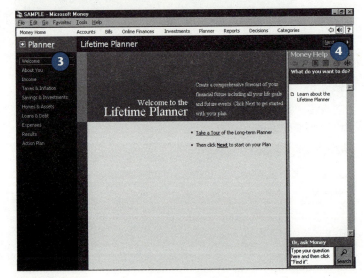

Average annual returns.
*The Lifetime Planner asks
what investment return you
expect. You may be interested
in knowing, therefore, that
common stocks have averaged
about 10.5 percent over the
last 70 years, while long-term
bonds have averaged about 5
to 6 percent, and small
company stocks have averaged
12.5 percent. These are gross
return numbers. Your return
would be reduced by any
investment expenses you pay.*

Income tax rates. *The
Lifetime Planner asks you
about the income tax and
inflation rates you expect. You
should experiment with a
variety of tax and inflation
rates to see how sensitive your
plans are to changes in these
important variables.*

**Navigating within the
Wizard.** *You can move
backward to a previous dialog
box by clicking the Previous
button. You can then move
forward, predictably, by
clicking the Next button. The
Previous and Next buttons
appear in the upper-right
corner of the window.*

6 To continue through the
Lifetime Planner, click
Next.

7 When you finish the planning process, choose the
File menu's Print com-
mand to print a paper
copy of your plan.

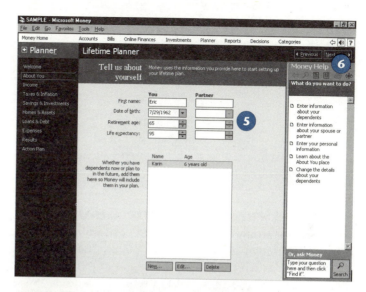

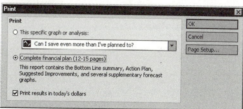

6

Tips for Retirement Planning

Before you determine how much you need to save to reach your retirement income goal, you need to set a goal for yourself and also see how much you can save in employer pension plans.

Set a Retirement Income Goal

People throw around all sorts of rules of thumb about this figure. In my case, for example, I figure that I want to live pretty much the same way when I'm retired as I do right now. Of course, when I'm retired, I won't have to make my mortgage payment—my mortgage will have long since been paid by then. And I won't have to pay Social Security or Medicare taxes—you only pay Social Security and Medicare taxes on earned income, not on unearned income, which is what retirement income is. I also won't have the work expenses, such as work clothes and commuting costs, that I now have. So if I take my current income and subtract my mortgage payment, my Social Security and Medicare taxes, and my work expenses, I get a retirement income number that lets me live the same way I do now. Note that if you live in a big house but plan on moving to a small condominium, for example, you can reduce your retirement income goal even more.

The basic calculations you make for determining your retirement income are as follows:

1 Look at your current income.

2 Adjust it for expenses you won't have once you're retired.

The caution I'll give, however, is that you don't want to be too optimistic about reducing your expenses. It's pretty safe to assume that you won't have a mortgage payment when you retire at age 62 if, for example, your mortgage will be paid off by age 59. And while no one knows how the tax laws will change between now and the time you retire, I also think it's pretty safe to assume that your retirement income won't be subject to Social Security and Medicare taxes. But I'd be cautious about assuming you can, for example, tighten up your living expenses, or get by with just one car if you and your spouse now drive two.

Consider Employer Pension Plans

As you consider strategies for saving money for retirement, I should say that there is one wildcard here—your employer's pension plan. I think you can probably rely on your employer's pension plan. And it just may be that your employer's pension plan will provide you with all the retirement income you need. But you need to be careful.

One factor that you need to worry about a little is whether your retirement income benefits depend on your continued employment. Let me explain.

One kind of retirement plan, called a *defined benefit plan,* pays you retirement income based on your salary in the final year or years you worked. With this type of plan, for example, you might receive a pension benefit of $32,000 if you work 40 years for a big company and make $40,000 in your final year.

A defined benefit plan, such as the one I just described, can be a great deal for employees. In fact, if your employer has a plan like this and you can be sure of some day receiving the benefits, you probably don't need to save a dime for retirement. No kidding.

But there's a problem with defined benefit plans if you work for a number of different employers instead of working for one employer for many years. This is true even if all the employers have the same "2 percent for every year you work" benefit formula.

The problem is that the figure on which your retirement income is based—your final year's or years' salary—will be very low for all but your last employer or two. Inflation causes this, of course. And so does the fact that people tend to make less in their early working years.

To see how this works, suppose that you work some place for 40 years, that you're making $40,000 a year in your final years, and that you receive a retirement benefit equal to 2 percent of your final salary for every year you worked. In this case, for your first 10 years of work you would get $8,000 of retirement income (10 × 2% × $40,000). This would be true even though you were probably making far less at that time.

Now consider the case of your neighbor. Let's say she had four different jobs over her working years. Let's say her first job, the one she worked during the first 10 years of her career, paid less because it was a less demanding job. And, of course, 30 years of inflation have passed since she left that job. So maybe her salary at the 10-year marker was $7,000. In this case, for her first 10 years of work she'll get a retirement benefit from that employer of $1,400 (10 × 2% × $40,000).

Do you see the scary part of this? You, for your first 10 years of work, accumulate $8,000 of retirement income, but your neighbor, for her first 10 years of work, accumulates $1,400. Your neighbor's situation is even worse if she switched jobs more frequently—say, every couple of years or so. If that was the case, because of the way that pension benefit calculations work, it's possible for your neighbor to have *no* retirement benefits at all for her first 10 years of work.

What I've just described is, in a nutshell, the problem with defined benefit retirement programs. They can be wonderful deals for long-term employees, but for people who switch jobs frequently, they don't amount to such a good deal. Please note, too, that even if you have the best of intentions about staying some place for your entire career, you can't really be sure you'll do this. Companies downsize. Industries decline. What you want to do with your life may change.

6

Planning for College

College costs vary widely by region, but generally speaking, four years at a public university cost almost $40,000. Four years at a private university cost about $80,000, and four years at a select private university cost close to $120,000. Despite the high costs of college, however, your kids can go. As long as you have an idea about what kind of college your child will attend, you can come up with a pretty good guess of how much you need to save. The Lifetime Planner includes a dialog box you can use to see how much college costs for just about any four-year college or university.

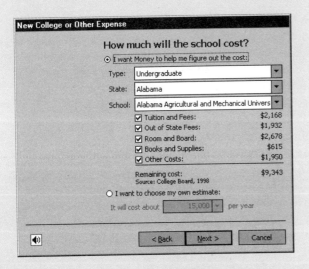

Investing College Savings

When you start saving money for your child's college expenses, you'll need to decide whose name to put on the savings account. You can hold the savings in your name, in which case you'll be taxed on the investment income the savings produce, or you can give the savings to your child, in which case your child will be taxed. In general, you pay less income tax by putting money in your child's name. If the child is 14 years old or younger, the first $650 or so of investment income is tax-free, and the next $650 is taxed at the lowest marginal income tax rate. If the child is 15 years old or older, the first $3,450 of income is tax-free (this might include both investment income and earned income if the child now has a job), and roughly the next $25,000 of income is taxed at the lowest marginal rate.

The one awkward thing about putting the money in a child's name is that the money really does become the child's. You can't borrow it temporarily—even if you have a good reason to do so. And when children reach the age of majority, either 18 or 21, they can spend the money on anything they want.

The other tricky thing about deciding whether to put the savings in the child's or in the parent's name has to do with current financial aid regulations. These regulations assume that basically all of a child's savings are available for college but that only a portion of his or her parent's savings are available.

Despite the risks, I recommend using a custodial account to save money for college expenses if you're going to initiate a long-term, substantial college savings program. If you're not going to initiate a long-term, substantial savings program, I'd say go ahead and keep the money in your name.

Where Should You Invest College Savings Money?

As long as you start early—preferably while your child is still in diapers and definitely not long after your child starts grade school—I think it makes sense to invest college savings money in the stock market. Go for something that's well-diversified and inexpensive. (A no-load stock index fund based on the Standard & Poors 500 is what I've got my kids' college money in.)

If you figure on the stock market delivering its historical average of 10 percent and you subtract about 0.2 percent for expenses, you can figure on your college savings money earning about 9.8 percent. That's pretty good.

Then, at some point in the future, you'll want to begin moving money from the stock market into something very safe. Some financial writers advocate moving money from stocks to short-term bonds or certificates of deposit four to five years before you need it. This means moving a child's college freshman year money from the stock market to bonds at roughly the time the child is a high school freshman. Move more money into safer investments in each of the next three years to provide for the child's sophomore, junior, and senior years of college.

6

What to Do If You Can't Afford College

Even if you can't afford a dime for your kid's college education, your kids can still figure out a way to go to college and even on to graduate and professional school. They will have to be a bit more flexible. They may need to be a bit more creative. But with some work and planning—and perhaps, more important, the desire—any kid can go to college. It's more important to offer emotional support and encouragement than cold, hard cash.

For this reason, don't worry if you can only save, say, 50 or 75 percent of what your calculations show as necessary. If you can just start saving money regularly—especially if you start early—you can make wonderful progress.

Let me also mention that I have several friends who successfully and solely paid their ways through both college and graduate and professional school. They all describe the experience as positive and a source of real pride. But enough said. Let's look at the down-and-dirty mechanics of saving serious money.

Basically, saving for college comes down to reducing either of the variables in the following formula:

Annual College Costs × Years of College =
Total College Costs

If you start brainstorming, you can quickly come up with a lot of good ideas for reducing the costs of college.

In the lists that follow, I describe the best ways I know of to reduce annual college costs as well as the number of years it takes to complete college.

Here are ways to reduce the cost of going to college:

◆ Attend a community college for the first two years rather than a public university. This saves $8,000 over the first two years.

◆ Attend an equivalent public university instead of a private university. This can save tens of thousands of dollars over four years

◆ Live at home rather than in student housing and attend a college as a commuter student. Your savings with this tactic are about $1,200 a year (the net of commuting costs).

◆ Get a part-time student job, such as a dormitory resident assistant. This saves $3,000 (usually paid as free room and board).

◆ Do a one-quarter work-for-credit study that pays a real salary. This saves $3,000 in earnings during the quarter.

◆ Work at the college as a full-time employee. Many colleges will then allow you to take a part-time class load for free or for a nominal fee.

Here are ways to reduce the amount of time spent in college:

◆ Take Advanced Placement (AP) classes in high school. (If your child's high school doesn't offer Advanced Placement classes, you can also arrange for College Level Examination Program, or CLEP, examinations.) Many high schools offer half a dozen AP classes, and some offer twice that many.

◆ Take a transferable community college class during the summer breaks. You can shave off one quarter or even a semester this way.

◆ Take an extra class a year. Or take an extra class each quarter or semester if you can take the extra class for free.

I know that some of the tricks and techniques included in the two preceding lists aren't exactly appealing. But if someone has to choose between going to college on a shoe-string budget or not going at all, college on a shoe-string budget is the better choice, by far.

Applying for Financial Aid

To determine whether a student is eligible for financial aid, you fill out the Free Application for Federal Student Aid, or FAFSA. The information you provide on this statement determines the amount the government and colleges expect you to contribute to your child's educa-tional expenses. The financial aid formulas expect you to live at the poverty line—about $15,000 for a family of four—and then contribute between 10 and 20 percent of the income you make in excess of the poverty line to your child's college expenses. Your child is expected to earn and contribute about $1,000 per year and pay whatever savings he or she has toward the expense of college. Whatever amount is left over after deducting these amounts determines the amount of financial aid for which the student is eligible.

Financial aid comes in three types: grants, loans, and work study programs. Grants are "free money" that doesn't need to be repaid, but are available to only the neediest of students. College loans are much more prevalent, and loans are available in several forms. Some loans are given to parents, while others are given to students. Some loans are through a bank, while others come directly from the federal government. Some loans are need-based and do not require you to pay interest on the loan until the student graduates from college, while other loans are unsubsidized and not based on need. Last, work study programs allow qualified students to help pay for their college costs by working for an approved employer, often on campus. To find out more about financial aid programs available at the college your child plans on attending, inquire at the college's financial aid office.

6

Using the Debt Reduction Planner

Another useful personal financial planning feature available within Money 99 Financial Suite is the Debt Reduction Planner. The Debt Reduction Planner allows you to map out a detailed plan for repaying all your debts—credit card, consumer loans (like those for a car or boat), and even a mortgage.

Run the Debt Reduction Planner

1 Click Planner on the navigation bar.

2 Click the Debt Reduction Planner hyperlink.

3 Review the loan and credit card accounts listed in the Debt Plan.

4 If you see an account listed in the Debt Plan that shouldn't be there, click the account and then click the Move Out Of Plan button. When Money asks you to confirm your decision, press Enter.

5 If you see an account that isn't included in the Debt Plan but should be, click the account and then click the Move Into Plan button. When Money asks you to specify what size payment you want to make on the debt, enter the payment amount in the Amount To Be Paid field.

6 If you notice a loan or credit card account missing from the list in the Debt Plan, click the New Account button. Then run the Wizard that Money starts to describe the debt and set up an account.

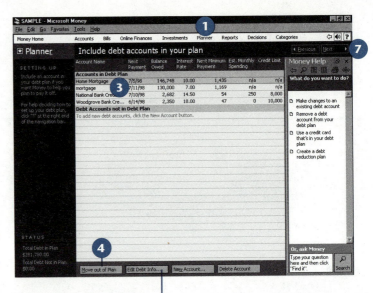

If you see a loan or credit card account with incorrect information, select the account and click this button to run a Wizard and correct the debt and account description.

TRY THIS

Navigating within the Wizard. *You can move backward to a previous dialog box by clicking the Previous button. You can then move forward, predictably, by clicking the Next button. The Previous and Next buttons appear in the upper-right corner of the window.*

7 Click the Next button to define your payment plan.

8 If you want to define your payment plan by saying that you want to make a specified payment, mark the What I Want To Pay Each Month button, and then use the slider buttons to set the payment amount. Note that you can also set a one-time payment amount.

9 If you want to define your payment plan by saying that you want to get out of debt by a specified date, mark the Date I Want To Be Out Of Debt button, and then use the slider buttons to set the deadline date.

10 Click Next. Money displays a line chart that graphically depicts your debt reduction plan.

11 Click Next. Then, optionally, schedule the payments required for your debt reduction plan.

12 Click Finish.

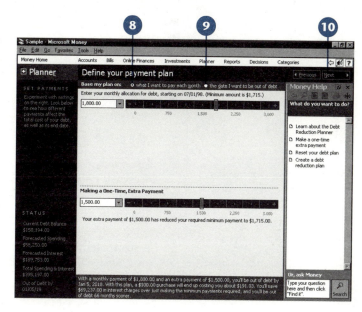

6

Using the Budget Planner

The best way to arrange your day-to-day financial affairs is to summarize how you spend your income and then create guidelines for your spending. Most people call this "budgeting." Once you've decided how you will budget your income and expenses, recording that budget with Money is simple. All you do is describe how much you'll earn or spend in each income or expense category.

TRY THIS

Produce one of Money's Spending Habit reports to use as a guideline in your budgeting. Section 5, "Creating Reports and Charts," describes how you produce reports.

Run the Budget Planner

1 Click Planner on the navigation bar.

2 Click the Budget Planner hyperlink.

3 Click the Next button.

4 Follow the on-screen instructions, paying particular attention to the contents of the Money Help window. When Money displays the Income tab, for example, use it to identify which categories of income you'll receive and the deposits you'll record.

5 Using the Previous and Next buttons, continue to move through the Long-Term Savings, Occasional Expense Fund, Debt, and Expenses tabs. Follow the on-screen instructions for completing the budget-planning tasks associated with each tab.

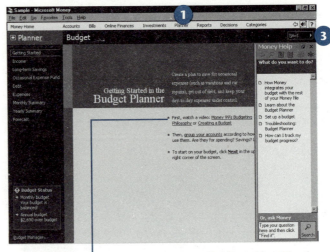

You may want to take the time to view a budget video. They're very helpful if this is the first time you're budgeting with Money.

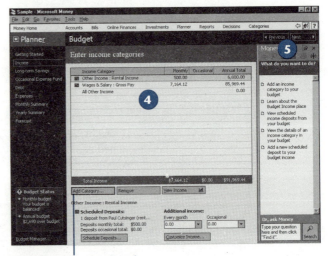

To add a new category of income not shown, click the Add Category button.

TIP

If you have Money 99 Basic, you can click Budget on the navigation bar to build a simple budget.

TIP

Navigating within the Wizard. *You can move backward to a previous dialog box by clicking the Previous button. You can then move forward, predictably, by clicking the Next button. The Previous and Next buttons appear in the upper-right corner of the window.*

⑥ When you reach the Month Summary tab, review the monthly budget information for accuracy and reasonableness, and then click Next.

⑦ When you reach the Yearly Summary tab, again, review the annual budget information for accuracy and reasonableness, and then click Next.

⑧ Review the Forecast tab for a detailed graphic view of your budget.

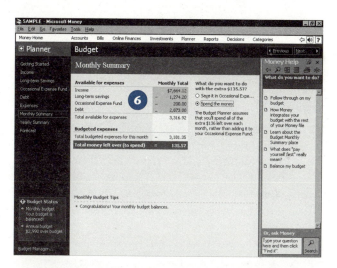

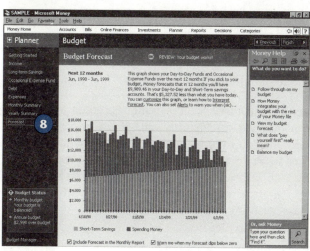

Six Ways to Stretch Your Budget Dollars

Take Aim at Your Biggest Expenses

If you've been working with Money for any length of time, produce a spending habits report and look at your three largest spending categories. (These spending categories probably constitute most of your spending.) Next, sit down with your family and brainstorm about ways to reduce these expenses.

What you're doing here is only rational. It's much easier to carve out $25 a month of savings in a category in which you're spending $500 a month than it is in a category in which you're spending $50 a month. To save $25 in a $500-a-month expense, you need to figure out how to shave off only 5 percent. To save $25 in a $50-a-month expense, you need to figure out how to chop off 50 percent.

Even if your three biggest spending categories are your housing, car, and grocery bills, if you want to find extra money, you're more likely to succeed by looking wherever you're currently spending the most money. Moving from a three bedroom apartment to a two bedroom apartment, for example, will save probably 10 percent or more on your housing expenses. So will moving into a smaller house.

If a housing change is too traumatic, consider driving a less-expensive, more gas-efficient car or taking the bus. Try to arrange a car pool. If your family uses two cars, consider getting rid of one.

Live Healthier

Here's a strange coincidence. If you make healthy lifestyle choices, you usually save money. Quit smoking, for example, and you easily add $30 or $40 to your monthly cash flow. If you're a heavy smoker, you could add even more. Moderate your alcohol consumption or quit drinking alcohol, and you can save just as much money each month. And there are the less obvious healthy choices: drinking less coffee, eating less meat, cutting down on sweets, walking or biking rather than driving.

To find out where you are spending money on bad habits, keep a record of where you spend each and every dollar for a few days. Then look at the list. The following table shows a sample list along with the annual cost of the habit.

ITEM	COST	POSSIBLE YEARLY SAVINGS
Specialty morning coffee	$1.75	$437.50 (if every working day of year)
Cookie after lunch	$0.90	$225.00 (if every working day of year)
Cigarettes	$3.00	$1,095.00 (if pack-a-day smoker)
Six-pack after work	$5.00	$520.00 (if two six-packs a week)

Think Green

If you're environmentally conscious, you can also save money. And probably quite a lot. Don't drive if you can walk. Turn your thermostat down a few degrees. Shorten your showers. Turn lights and appliances off when you're not using them. By participating more fully in recycling and composting you can almost eliminate garbage bills. Take good care of your car and make the necessary repairs, and you may be able to drive it for 200,000 miles and keep it out of the junkyard for an extra 10 years. If you don't have prejudices about second-hand goods, you can purchase just about anything—clothing, furniture, cars—at great savings. By becoming less of a consumer, you save money and are kind to Mother Earth at the same time.

Stop Using Your Credit Card

Research suggests that people spend about 23 percent more on purchases when they shop with a credit card. If you then pay 15 percent or 20 percent interest on the money you've borrowed with your credit card, you end up paying almost 50 percent more for everything.

Given the propensity to spend more with credit cards, one thing you can probably do to save money is stop using your credit card. If you're skeptical about this gambit, by the way, just try it for a week or two. You may find yourself buying less expensive lunches and not purchasing certain items altogether.

Find One Expense That Wastes Money

Without knowing the specifics of your situation, I suspect you have one or two expenses that, if you didn't make them, would not affect your life at all. For example, do you subscribe to magazines that you never get around to reading? Do you pay to store a boat, an RV, an antique car, or a motorcycle 12 months of the year and only bring it out to enjoy once or twice a year? Consider pulling the plug on the expense. While there probably is some emotional reason for making the expenditure, cutting these kinds of expenses doesn't affect your standard of living.

Find One Expense That You're Willing to Compromise

Another tactic that makes sense is to compromise some area of your spending. Decide right now that you're going to find an area where you will make do with less by living frugally or by making small sacrifices. Then go out and pick the one expenditure in your budget that means the very least to you. Maybe it's athletic club dues. Or the premium cable television stations. This sounds silly, but it usually works. It's often difficult to decide to save, say, $1.00 a day, but it's easier to decide to save a dollar a day by not stopping for coffee on the way to work any more.

6

Using the Home Worksheet

The Home Worksheet lets you estimate what price home you can afford based on both your income and your existing debt, calculating what size home or what size mortgage payment you can afford.

⊞ Decisions

Estimate Home Affordability

1 Click Decisions on the navigation bar.

2 Click the Tools hyperlink.

3 Click the Home Worksheet hyperlink.

4 Click the Information tab.

5 Use the Calculate field to indicate what you want to calculate: the cash you'll spend, the monthly payment you'll make, the purchase price, or some combination of these variables.

6 Use the Information tab's fields to describe the home purchase in as much detail as you can. Note that you don't have to fill a field you've told Money to calculate.

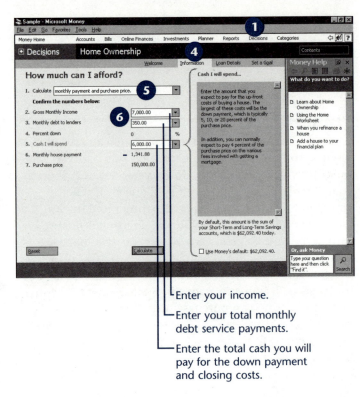

Enter your income.

Enter your total monthly debt service payments.

Enter the total cash you will pay for the down payment and closing costs.

Calculate a debt-to-income ratio. *The Decisions Center provides a tool you can use to estimate your debt-to-income ratio. To use this tool, click Decisions on the navigation bar, click the Tools hyperlink, and then click the Debt Ratio Calculator.*

7 Click the Loan Details tab.

8 Use the Loan Details tab's fields to describe the mortgage you'll use. Note that Money supplies its best guesses for most of the variables.

9 Click the Set A Goal tab to see a snapshot summary of your home affordability calculations.

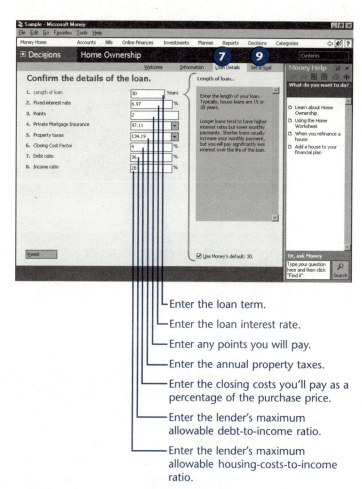

Enter the loan term.

Enter the loan interest rate.

Enter any points you will pay.

Enter the annual property taxes.

Enter the closing costs you'll pay as a percentage of the purchase price.

Enter the lender's maximum allowable debt-to-income ratio.

Enter the lender's maximum allowable housing-costs-to-income ratio.

6

Using the Decision Center

Money's Decision Center actually provides three sets of tools: articles, calculators, and worksheets. There isn't room in this book to describe in detail all three sets of tools—I'm only covering the worksheets in detail. Nevertheless, you'll find the Decision Center both interesting and useful. So I want to quickly describe it here.

Reviewing the Decision Center Articles

The Decision Center provides general articles on a variety of personal financial planning topics. To access these articles, you click Decisions on the navigation bar and then click the tab (other than the Tools tab) that corresponds to a category of personal financial-planning articles. (For example, if you want to see a list of articles about saving money, click the Saving tab.) Then you click the article you want to read. (For example, to learn about how to set up an emergency fund, click Priority 1: Set Up An Emergency Fund.)

When Money displays the article, read it online, using the Page Up and Page Down keys to scroll through the text. Note, too, that you can choose the File menu's Print command to print a paper copy of the article. And one interesting thing to watch for: within Decision Center articles, you'll find hyperlinks that point to Internet resources such as the Moneyinsider Web site at *www.moneyinsider.com.*

Reviewing the Decision Center Calculators

The Decision Center provides fourteen calculators: Tuition Savings, Debt Ratio, Tax Deduction Finder, Can You Deduct Your IRA?, Savings, Debt Consolidation, Tax Relief Act, Buy vs. Rent, Comparing Mortgages, Life Insurance, The Tax Bite, Figuring Your Retirement Expenses, Retirement Income, and Risk Tolerance Quiz.

The Decision Center calculators all use self-descriptive names. The Tuition Savings Calculator, for example, estimates how much you'll need to save for a child's college costs and also how much college might cost in the future. The Debt Ratio Calculator calculates what percentage of your income you spend on debt payments and then assesses the reasonableness of this ratio in light of a prospective lender's underwriting standards.

The Decision Center calculators are easy to use. They each start a simple wizard you use to make a useful calculation—such as how much you should save for a child's future college costs. The figure on the next page, for example, shows the first window used by the Tuition Savings Calculator.

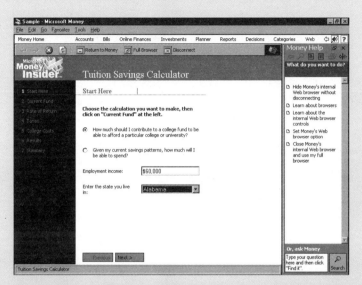

To use one of the Calculator Wizards, you simply fill in the blanks and click buttons. Most calculators require you to complete several steps. You do that by clicking the Next button. You can return to a previous step—say you need to make a change—by clicking the Previous button.

Reviewing the Decision Center Worksheets

The Decision Center also provides four, powerful worksheets: Home, Loan, Home Inventory, and Tax. The Decision Center Worksheets, which are described in the two pages that precede this sidebar and the six pages

that follow it, collect more data and do more with the data compared with Decision Center calculators.

The Home Worksheet, for example, lets you estimate what price home you can afford based on both your income and your existing debt. To use this worksheet, you simply describe your current financial condition and, in financial terms, the home you want to consider buying. The Home Worksheet then calculates what size home or what size mortgage payment you can afford. Although this worksheet isn't difficult to use, you'll want to spend a few minutes working with it in order to get comfortable.

The Loan Worksheet lets you analyze an individual loan and compare loan alternatives. To use this worksheet, you describe the loan or loans you're considering in precise terms. The worksheet then calculates the loan payments and total costs.

The Home Inventory Worksheet lets you build a list of all your personal property. You might do this if you want to build a record of valuable assets you've insured. To use this worksheet, first click the window tab that corresponds to a category of personal property (such as appliances). Then click the New button and use the dialog box that Money displays to describe the asset.

The Tax Worksheet lets you estimate what you'll pay in income taxes for the year. To use this worksheet, you describe your filing status, income, and deductions. This easy-to-use tool, by the way, can be a financial lifesaver if your income and deductions make it impossible for you to estimate your income taxes.

6

Using the Loan Worksheet

The Loan Worksheet lets you analyze and compare loan alternatives. To use this worksheet, you describe the loan or loans you're considering in precise terms. The worksheet then calculates the loan payments and total costs.

Loan Planner

Analyze a Loan

1 Click Decisions on the navigation bar.

2 Click the Tools hyperlink.

3 Click the Loan Worksheet hyperlink.

4 Click the Initial Costs tab.

5 Use the Initial Costs tab's fields to describe the loan or loans you're considering.

6 Click the Loan Terms tab.

7 Use the I Want Money To Calculate field to indicate what you want to calculate: the length of the loan, the principal and interest, the loan amount, the starting interest rate, or the balloon payment amount.

8 Use the other fields to describe the loan or loans in greater detail. Note that you don't have to provide the loan variable you want Money to calculate.

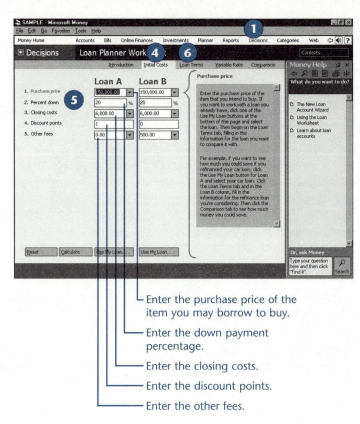

Enter the purchase price of the item you may borrow to buy.

Enter the down payment percentage.

Enter the closing costs.

Enter the discount points.

Enter the other fees.

Adjustable rate mortgages. *If you want to analyze an adjustable rate, or variable rate, mortgage, click the Loan Worksheet's Variable Rate tab. Then use its fields to describe the variable rate loan you're considering.*

9 Click the Calculate button to calculate the variable you didn't supply.

10 Click the Comparison tab to display an analysis of the loan or loans you're considering.

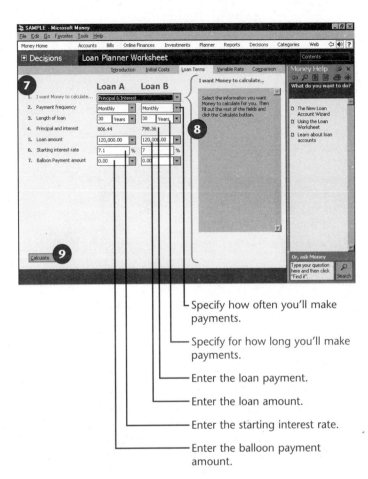

Specify how often you'll make payments.

Specify for how long you'll make payments.

Enter the loan payment.

Enter the loan amount.

Enter the starting interest rate.

Enter the balloon payment amount.

6

Using the Home Inventory Worksheet

The Home Inventory Worksheet lets you build a list of all your personal property. You might do this if you want to build a record of valuable assets you've insured.

Inventory Your Household Items

1 Click Decisions on the navigation bar.

2 Click the Tools hyperlink.

3 Click the Home Inventory hyperlink.

4 Click the New button.

5 Click the down arrow at the end of the Asset Type field, and select an asset group description from the list.

6 Enter a brief description of the item in the Description field.

7 Use the Location field to indicate where you've stored the item or where you use it.

8 Use the Current Value, Replacement Value, and Purchase Price fields to describe what you originally paid for the item—and what you estimate it would cost to replace the item. You can also use the Purchase Date and Purchased At fields for further documentation.

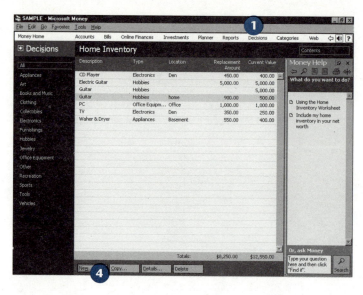

Copy items to save time.

To quickly enter several similiar items, you can copy an item's description that you've already entered. Just select the item and then click the Copy button. When you do this, Money copies the description of the selected item and then opens the Inventory Details dialog box, filling its fields with the copied data.

9 Optionally, provide additional information about the item such as the model and make and serial number.

10 Click Enter. Money adds the item to the Home Inventory.

11 Repeat steps 4 through 10 for each of the items you want to add to the home inventory.

12 Choose the File menu's Print command to print a paper copy of the Home Inventory worksheet.

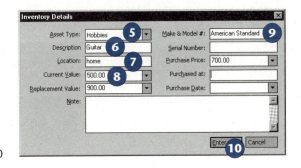

6

Using the Tax Worksheet

The Tax Worksheet lets you estimate what you'll pay in income taxes for the year. To use this worksheet, you describe your filing status, income, and deductions. This easy-to-use tool, by the way, can be a financial lifesaver if your income and deductions make it impossible for you to estimate your income taxes.

Estimate Income Tax Expense

1 Click Decisions on the navigation bar.

2 Click the Tools hyperlink.

3 Click the Tax Worksheet hyperlink.

4 Click the Overview tab. Then use its fields to describe your filing status, number of dependents, other deductions, spouse deduction, the year for which you're estimating taxes, and the estimated taxes already paid.

5 Click the Income tab. Then use its fields to describe your income, including your wages and salary, interest and dividends, capital gains, alimony you receive, unemployment, and other income items.

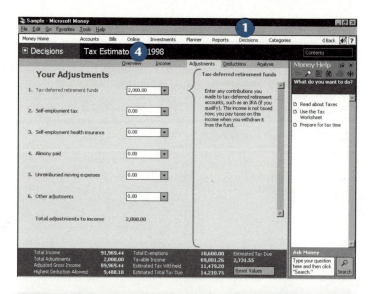

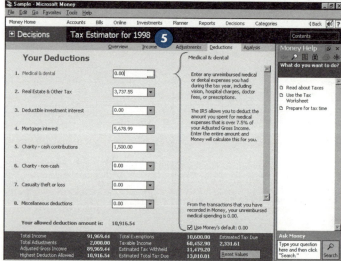

*To display Money's analysis of
your Tax Worksheet
calculations, click the Analysis
tab. The Analysis tab also
provides tax and penalty
saving tips.*

6 Click the Adjustments tab.
Then use its fields to describe any adjustments for
adjusted gross income,
including any contribu-
tions to tax-deferred re-
tirement accounts (such
as an Individual Retire-
ment Account), self-em-
ployment taxes and
medical insurance deduc-
tions, alimony you pay,
unreimbursed moving
expenses, and other ad-
justments.

7 Click the Deductions tab.
Then use its fields to describe any itemized de-
ductions you are allowed,
including medical and
dental expenses, real es-
tate and property taxes,
deductible investment
interest, mortgage inter-
est, charitable contribu-
tions, casualty and theft
losses, and miscellaneous
deductions.

8 To see your estimated
income tax expenses,
review the summary
information at the bottom
of the Tax Worksheet
window.

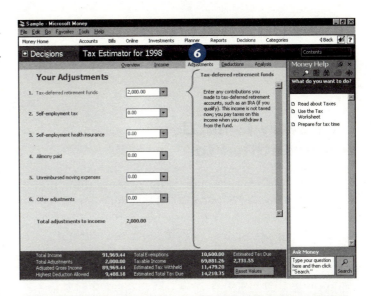

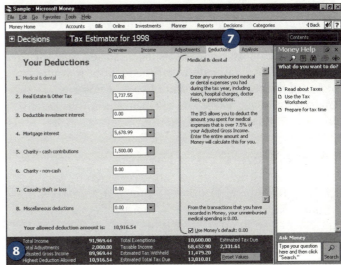

The Four Best Ways to Save Money on Taxes

Take Every Deduction You're Entitled to

I continually run into people who don't take all the deductions they're entitled to. Some of them think they increase their risk of being audited by taking too many deductions. Others think maybe they're being a little unpatriotic by taking too many deductions. But not taking every deduction you're entitled to is a big mistake. The U.S. Congress writes the tax laws with the assumption that taxpayers will take every deduction to which they're entitled.

If you routinely give away clothing your kids have outgrown to the local thrift shop, for example, be sure to collect a receipt, assign a fair value, and then take the amount as a charitable donation deduction. If you're spending money on night school so that you can acquire new skills and get better job, take the amount as an employee business expense deduction.

Bunch Your Deductions

Perhaps the best way to save money on income taxes without giving up anything in return is to bunch your deductions so that you take the standard deduction in some years and itemize deductions in other years. This effectively increases your deductions. Let me explain. Let's say you're married and that you routinely have about $8,000 a year in itemized deductions.

Furthermore, just to make the math simple, let's also assume that you can take a $7,000 standard deduction. In any given year, then, it makes sense to take the $8,000 a year in itemized deductions because that reduces your income tax bill. But if you pay some deductions early and some deductions late, you can actually increase the total deductions you're taking over time. Why? Because (and this is the trick) in the years when your itemized deductions fall below the standard deduction amount, you can take the standard deduction. Let me show you how this works over a four-year time frame.

Let's say that your plan is to use the standard $7,000 deduction in years 1 and 3 and itemized deductions in years 2 and 4. In this case, you want to pay as many of your deductions as you can in years 2 and 4. The table below shows an example of what your itemized deductions could be in years 1, 2, 3, and 4 if you did this kind of juggling.

ITEMIZED DEDUCTION	YEAR 1	YEAR 2	YEAR 3	YEAR 4
Mortgage interest	$5,500	$6,500	$5,000	$7,000
Real estate taxes	0	$3,000	0	$3,000
Charitable donations	0	$2,000	0	$2,000
Total	$5,500	$11,500	$5,000	$12,000

Because you get to choose whether to itemize or use the standard deduction, you itemize in years 2 and 4, but you take the standard deduction in years 1 and 3. If you itemize in each of the four years, you'll have $32,000 of deductions (four years times $8,000 a year). If you simply take the standard deduction, you'll have $28,000 of deductions (four years times $7,000). But by bunching your deductions and then flip-flopping between the standard deduction and itemized deductions, you can deduct $37,500.

Exploit Retirement Savings Options

Tax-deferred investment options such as 401(k)s, 403(b)s, IRAs, SEP/IRAs, and Keoghs are such good deals that I can't promote them enough. If you're saving for retirement (and you should be), these tax-deferred investment options are absolutely the best way to go.

Don't Use Nondeductible Consumer Credit

Another very powerful tax-savings gambit is to convert nondeductible consumer credit interest on items such as car loans, credit cards, personal lines of credit, and so forth to deductible mortgage or home equity loan interest. To do this, you need to be a homeowner, of course. But assuming you are, you could take out, say, a $25,000 second mortgage home equity loan and use the proceeds to pay off your car loan, all your credit cards, a student loan you're still paying on, and any other debts you have.

If you swap $25,000 of consumer credit that charges 10 percent interest with a $25,000 home equity loan that charges 10 percent, for example, you still pay $2,500 a year of interest, but you can use the $2,500 of home equity loan interest as a deduction. If your marginal, or highest, income tax rate is 28 percent, you save about $700 a year. If the home equity loan's interest rate happens to be lower than the average interest rate you're paying on all the consumer credit you replace—and it probably is—you save even more money.

Despite the substantial savings available, I caution you regarding this particular gambit, especially if you're someone who likes to use a credit card. Sure, if you do one of these home equity loan things and use the proceeds to pay off your consumer credit debt, it may save on taxes. But you won't be in any better shape if you go out and start charging up your credit cards again. More than a few people take out a home equity loan and then find themselves with both a $25,000 home equity loan and a bunch of new credit card debts.

Let me mention one other problem: you could end up stretching out the repayment of your debt. Swapping a deductible home equity loan for a nondeductible car loan sounds like a good idea. And it really may save on taxes. But you might not get ahead if your car loan has 3 years of payments left and your new home equity loan lets you make payments over the next 10 years.

6

Tracking Assets and Liabilities

Microsoft Money's strength lies in keeping records of financial assets such as bank accounts, money-market funds, and investments, as well as in tracking liabilities such as mortgages and credit cards. But besides tracking these sorts of assets and liabilities, you can also use Money to track whatever else you own. And using Money for all detailed and thorough financial record-keeping can deliver enormous benefits.

If you're a homeowner, for example, you can keep a record of the improvements you've made to your home—and that can save on taxes later. By monitoring the money you borrow and what that money costs you (in interest), you can do a much better job of planning and managing your day-to-day financial affairs. You'll also be able to calculate your net worth more accurately—and that can lead to better personal financial-planning decisions.

Creating Asset Accounts

To track your net worth, you set up asset accounts for each major asset you own: your house, the car or cars you drive, and any other large, valuable items. You may also want to set up a catchall account for tracking the items that perhaps aren't especially valuable individually but collectively add up to a significant value, things such as baseball cards or silverware.

TIP

If you're setting up an asset account for a house, enter the house's original cost.

Create an Asset Account

1 Click Accounts on the navigation bar to display the Account Manager window.

2 Click the New Account button.

3 Click the Not Held At A Financial Institution option button, and click Next.

4 Select Asset from the list, and click Next.

5 Enter a name for the asset account, and click Next.

6 Enter the current value of the asset or its original cost, and click Next.

7 Specify whether a loan account is associated with the asset account by clicking the Yes or No option button, and click Next.

8 If you indicated that a loan account is associated with the asset account, click the down arrow in the Loan Account field and select the loan account from the list.

9 Click Finish.

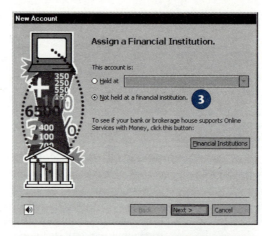

Tracking Assets

Once you've set up an asset account, it isn't difficult to keep a record of the asset and track the changes in its value. As with recording a check in a bank account register, you use the transaction forms at the bottom of the Account Register window to track changes to the value of an asset.

TRY THIS

If you're recording an increase in value, Money objects if you attempt to use an expense category to categorize the transaction. To avoid this problem, you can create a category to describe depreciation and appreciation of assets by entering Market Adjustment *in the Category field.*

Track an Asset

1. Display the register for the asset account.

2. Click the Decrease or Increase tab, depending on whether you're describing a negative or positive change in the asset's value.

3. Enter the date of the change.

4. Optionally, enter the name of the person or business you paid if you made improvements on the asset.

5. Enter the amount of the change.

6. Click the down arrow in the Category field, and select an expense category.

7. Optionally, enter a description of the change in the Memo field

8. Click Enter to record the increase or decrease and recalculate the asset account's balance.

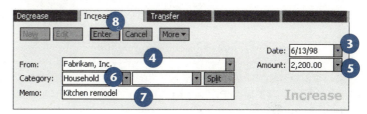

Tips for Tracking Assets

Asset accounts work very much like bank accounts, and the mechanics of keeping track of an asset with Money are straightforward. Asset record-keeping, however, can be a little tricky.

Your Home

A home is usually a person's single largest asset. If you own a home and have decided to track your net worth with Money, you'll want to set up a home, or personal residence, account and use it to track the value of your home.

The historical appreciation of real estate makes it tempting to track the fair market value of a home. However, it may make more sense to track the original cost of the home as well as the cost of any home improvements. Although current income regulations exempt the first $250,000 of capital gain on the sale of a primary residence ($500,000 if married), homeowners who hold the same property for long periods of time and then enjoy steady appreciation can still exceed these limits. For example, a single taxpayer who purchases a $150,000 home and then experiences 4 percent inflation will have unrealized capital gains of roughly $330,000 thirty years in the future!

Even if you think that you won't own a home for the long time necessary to accumulate large, unrealized capital gains, you may still want to keep a record of your home's cost as well as the cost of improvements you make to it. There's no harm in doing so, the work is extremely minimal, and you might someday save a lot of money if tax laws change again.

To keep a record of a home's cost and the cost of improvements, you first set up an asset account named something like "Home" or "Residence." (I described how to do this on page 98.) In this account, you record as transactions the original cost of the home as well as associated purchase costs such as escrow fees and title insurance. In the future, whenever you spend money to improve your home, you transfer the money from your checking account to the asset account set up for your home.

What qualifies as an improvement? Anything that adds value to a home or to its useful life. For example, adding a swimming pool, finishing the basement, and landscaping the site all qualify as improvements. However, maintenance costs such as those for painting the exterior or interior, repairing a leaky roof, or fixing faulty electrical wiring don't qualify as improvements.

The only problem to this approach is that your financial records don't show the value of your home—only the total of its cost and any improvements. If you want to also show the home's value, you can add a transaction to your asset register that adjusts the account's total to the home's market value. Just be sure to delete this transaction before you calculate the capital gain stemming from the sale of the home

Cars, Boats, and Other Personal Property

Cars, boats, and other valuable personal property can usually be handled nicely with individual accounts. In general, you don't need to make a lot of adjustments to the value of these assets. And you probably won't make improvements that increase their value, anyway. So you may just want to periodically—say, at the end of each year—update the account balances so that the asset's ending balance approximates its fair market value.

Asset Lists for Property and Casualty Insurance

It's not a bad idea to maintain records of the assets you've insured with a property insurance policy. The reason for this is probably clear: if disaster strikes, a list of the insured items can make claim reports and collections easier and more complete.

If you have Money 99 Financial Suite, you can create this list using the Home Inventory Worksheet, which is described on pages 90–91. If you don't have Money 99

Financial Suite, you can set up another asset account called something like "Personal Property" and carefully list all assets you've insured. The more information on your list, the better. If possible, include information such as model numbers and original costs. Remember that you can use the Split Transaction dialog box to store additional data. Another great way to create an asset list for insured personal property (such as the contents of your home) is to walk through your house with a video camera and record what's in each room. You can also provide narrative descriptions of the items you're filming as you shoot the video.

One other point. Your asset list won't do much good if your computer and all your backup disks or your video tape are lost in a fire or flood (or whatever casualty destroys or damages the property you've insured). For this reason, you should probably keep an up-to-date copy of your asset list in a secure place such as a safe-deposit box.

Setting Up Loan Accounts

Tracking a loan with Money is very easy, especially if you're already familiar and comfortable with tracking a bank account and you know how to transfer money between accounts. To begin tracking a loan, all you need to do is find the paperwork that describes the loan and its current balance (probably the last monthly statement) and then use the New Account Wizard to set up an account for the loan.

mortgage

TIP

If you're describing an adjustable rate mortgage, enter the date of the next adjustment and the length of the period between adjustments.

Create a Loan Account

1. Click Accounts on the navigation bar to display the Account Manager window.

2. Click the New Account button.

3. Enter the name of the bank or financial institution to whom you'll make your payments, and click Next.

4. Select Loan from the list, and click Next three times.

5. Click the Borrowing Money option button, and click Next.

6. Enter the loan name and the lender, and click Next.

7. Specify whether the loan is a fixed or adjustable rate mortgage, and click Next.

8. Specify whether you have already made payments on the loan, and click Next.

9. Enter the date when you made the first loan payment, and click Next twice.

10. Select a payment frequency from the drop-down list box, and click Next.

11. Select the option that corresponds to your interest calculation method, and click Next.

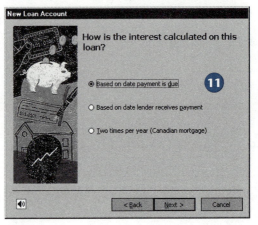

TIP

If you have made previous payments, Money asks how far back it should go to calculate the loan payments and amortization.

TIP

Be sure to enter the loan interest rate and not the annual percentage rate (APR) in the Interest Rate field.

TIP

How different loans calculate interest. *Interest on home mortgages is usually calculated based on the date the payment is due. Interest on most consumer credit loans, including car loans, is calculated based on the date the loan payment is received.*

TIP

If you have any other charges or fees you have to pay on the loan, such as property taxes or insurance premiums, click the Other Fees button and enter the fees in the Other Fees dialog box.

12 Enter four of the five loan calculation variables—the loan balance, the interest rate, the scheduled loan length, the combined principal and interest payment, and the balloon payment—in the dialog boxes Money provides. Click Next.

13 Click OK to accept the loan variable Money calculated for you, and then click Next twice to continue.

14 Specify which expense category you want to use to track the loan expense.

15 Specify whether the loan is a house loan, and click Next.

16 Specify whether the interest on this loan is tax-deductible, and click Next.

17 Enter the date you want to be reminded of the loan payment and the bank account from which you'll make the payment, and click Next.

18 Specify whether an asset account is associated with the loan. If so, select the asset account from the list box. Click Finish.

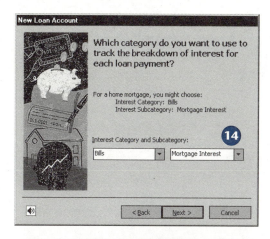

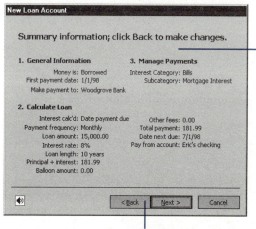

After you've entered all the loan account information, Money summarizes the loan.

If you discover you've made a mistake, click Back to backtrack your way through the New Loan Account Wizard's dialog boxes.

Setting Up Liability Accounts

If your loan won't be amortized, you set up a liability account instead of a loan account. Setting up a liability account works very much like setting up other accounts.

National Bank Liability

TIP

Loan amortization.
Amortization means that your loan payments include not only the interest but also the principal. Over time, as the principal payments reduce the loan's balance, more and more of each payment goes toward reducing the loan's balance. Conventional home mortgages and most car loans are amortizing loans.

Create a Liability Account

1. Click Accounts on the navigation bar to display the Account Manager window.

2. Click the New Account button.

3. Enter the name of the bank or financial institution to whom you'll make your payments, and click Next.

4. Select Liability from the list, and click Next.

5. Enter a name for the liability account, and click Next.

6. Enter the ending liability balance (the amount you still owe) from your last statement, and click Next.

7. Click the I Have No Other Accounts At This Institution option button, and click Next.

8. Click Finish.

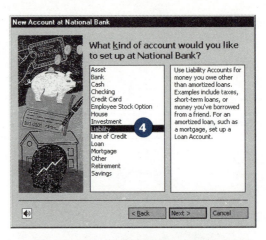

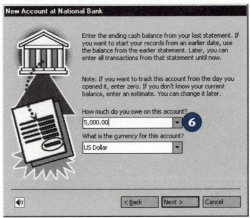

Entering Liability Account Payments

If you set up a liability account, you record in your checking account any check that pays interest or principal for the liability in the usual way.

TIP

Recording loan account payments. *You enter loan account payments in the same way you enter liability account payments. The only difference is that Money remembers the principal and interest breakdowns you provided when you set up the loan account, and so it enters most of the payment information for you.*

TIP

If you're recording a payment of principal only, you can use the Transfer tab.

Record a Liability Account Payment

1. Display the register for the checking account from which you want to write the liability account payment.

2. Click the Check tab (or the Withdrawal tab if the loan payment is automatically withdrawn from your account), and if necessary, click New.

3. Enter the check number.

4. Enter the check date.

5. Enter the lender's name in the Pay To field.

6. Enter the payment amount.

7. Describe the payment in the Category fields, or click the Split button to record a check that pays both interest and principal.

8. If you're splitting the transaction, use the Split Transaction dialog box to categorize each part of the transaction.

9. Click Enter to record the payment.

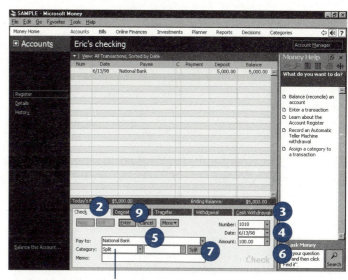

If you record a check that pays only interest, categorize it as an interest expense.

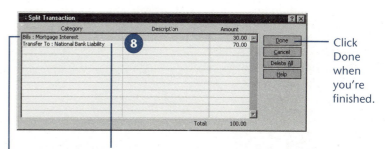

Click Done when you're finished.

Describe the principal part of the payment on the second line by recording a transfer to the liability account.

Describe the interest part of the payment on the first line, and categorize it as an interest expense.

Fixing Loan Account Balance Errors

Even though Money calculates the interest and principal portions of the loan payments you make, Money's calculations might still be wrong. This is especially true if the interest calculation is based on the date the payment is received by the lender. In this case, a delay in the mail of just a few days can create a difference in Money's calculation of the interest and the lender's calculation of the interest. Fortunately, it's easy to fix these kinds of errors.

Correct a Loan Account Balance

1. Display the register for the loan account.

2. Compare the ending balance for the account with whatever shows on the loan statement.

3. If your register balance varies from the loan statement, click Balance This Account on the Accounts bar.

4. Enter the ending balance from your monthly statement.

5. Enter the ending date from your monthly statement.

6. If any fees are not accounted for in your records, categorize the fees in the Category fields.

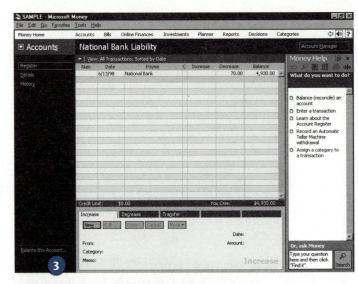

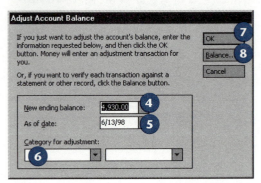

TIP

It's a good idea to balance your loan account each time you get a monthly statement.

SEE ALSO

For information about how the Balance Account Wizard works—and what to do when you can't get an account to balance—see pages 38–41.

7 If you want to manually adjust the loan account balance so that it matches the statement, click OK to adjust the balance.

8 If you want to balance the loan account in the same way that you balance checking accounts, click the Balance button. When you do, Money starts the Balance Account Wizard, which you can use to balance the loan account in the same way that you balance a bank account.

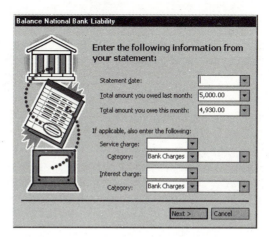

When to Repay and Refinance Mortgages

To determine whether it makes sense to repay a mortgage (or any other debt) early, you need to compare the interest rate the loan charges with the interest rate or investment return that some other investment pays. The rule is simple: your loan's interest rate needs to exceed the investment's interest rate or investment return in order for early loan repayment to make sense. If your mortgage charges 8 percent interest but you can buy a bond that pays 10 percent, for example, you shouldn't "invest" your money by repaying your mortgage early. You end up with more money by investing in the 10 percent bonds.

As a general rule, too, I should tell you that except in unusual situations (when your mortgage interest rate is in double-digits, for example), early mortgage repayment is probably not all that great a deal. If you can stick more money in your employer's 401(k) or 403(b) plan or in a tax-deductible individual retirement account (IRA), the 401(k), 403(b), or IRA always beats early mortgage repayment. In fact, it's not even a contest.

What About Your Other Debt?

While you get truly awesome interest savings when you look at the effect of repaying a long-term loan like a mortgage early, it's really a better deal to get out from under your credit card debt and other consumer credit debt.

Interest on consumer credit such as credit cards and car loans isn't tax-deductible. So a credit card that charges, say, 16 percent, really does cost 16 percent, whereas an 8 percent mortgage doesn't really cost 8 percent. Depending on your income tax situation, you get a tax deduction that effectively lowers your 8 percent mortgage to something between 5 percent and 7 percent. In effect, by paying off a credit card that charges a 16 percent interest rate, you make a 16 percent profit on your investment. (Your investment is paying off the credit card early.) If you pay off a mortgage that charges an effective, after-income-taxes-are-figured, interest rate of 5 percent, you make a 5 percent profit on your investment.

There's one other point that I should make about early repayment of debts. The idea is sound, but it doesn't really pay off if you go out and replace your old debt with new debt. Okay, that sounds funny. But let me explain. Paying off your mortgage early sounds like a great deal—and it is a great deal, really. But if you pay your mortgage off early and then, because you don't have mortgage payments, go out and purchase a new, larger, more expensive home, you're not really getting ahead. And if you get that credit card paid off early, but then you go out and fill your closet with a dazzling new wardrobe, you're not getting ahead that way either.

If you're paying a mortgage, it's easy to wonder whether you should refinance when interest rates drop. The logic seems straightforward enough: replace an expensive mortgage with a cheap mortgage and save money. Unfortunately, figuring out whether you'll actually save by refinancing a mortgage is very difficult.

Refinancing in a Nutshell

The trick to refinancing a mortgage is to make sure that you pay less for the new mortgage—taking into account both the interest charges and any refinancing costs— than you pay for your existing mortgage. To see if you pay less, you need to consider the interest rate and the refinancing costs, of course, but you also need to think about how long you'll be paying interest.

Fortunately, you can use the Decision Center's Comparing Mortgages tool, which is briefly described on page 86, to perform this analysis. You use the Comparing Mortgages tool generally as described in its online instructions, but with several minor twists.

When you describe your existing mortgage as the first mortgage (Mortgage A), don't worry about the loan fees and payments you've already made. For your existing mortgage, then, there aren't discount points, loan service fees, or closing costs. And for your existing mort-

gage, the loan balance and the scheduled loan length equal what is left for you to pay, not what you originally had to pay.

Does all that make sense? Think about it for a minute and it should. When you consider refinancing a loan, you basically compare two loans: your existing loan, for which you'll pay no extra discount points, no loan service fees, and no closing costs, and a new mortgage, for which you'll pay all these extra charges.

The Complicating Factor

Unfortunately, there's also a complicating factor when it comes to mortgage refinancing. If you want to refinance as a way to save money over the long haul, you shouldn't do it as a way to stretch out your payments. In other words, you're very unlikely to save money by replacing an existing mortgage that has 15 years of payments left with a new, refinanced mortgage that requires 30 years of payments. Even if the new mortgage's interest rate is much lower, you'll be borrowing the money for a lot longer with the new mortgage.

Investing in Stocks, Bonds, and Mutual Funds

Microsoft Money provides wonderful tools for investment record-keeping. If you're an investor, you've probably already considered whether and how to use Money to make investment record-keeping easier and less time-consuming.

In general, there are two good reasons for using Money to track your investments.

◆ Your investments affect your income taxes. If you have investments that aren't tax deferred, you need to track your investments with Money so that you know the taxable investment income that your investments produce and so you know about any capital gains or losses that occur (which will be taxable) when you sell an investment.

◆ You want to use Money's investment reports to assess the performance of your investments because you can't get annual investment return information somewhere else. By using Money's investment performance report, you can calculate the rate of return for the investments you're holding.

To get started with investment record-keeping, set up investment accounts and describe your current investment portfolio. After you complete these preliminary tasks, you can use Money for day-to-day financial record-keeping.

Setting Up Investment Accounts

To track your investments, set up at least one investment account. The general rule is to set up one investment account for each brokerage account statement you receive.

Investment Account

Set Up an Investment Account

1. Click Accounts on the navigation bar to display the Account Manager window.

2. Click the New Account button.

3. Optionally, enter the name of the financial institution associated with the account, and click Next.

4. Select Investment from the list of accounts, and click Next.

5. Enter a name for the investment account, and click Next.

6. Specify whether the account is tax deferred, and click Next.

7. Enter the estimated value of the investments in the account.

8. Specify whether the account has an associated cash account, and click Next.

If you're setting up one investment account for each monthly statement, you may want to provide the name of the mutual-fund management company or stock brokerage company.

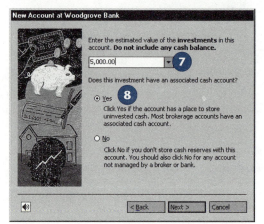

9 If the investment has an associated cash account, enter the cash account's ending balance from your last monthly statement and click Next.

10 Select the option that best corresponds with the way you use the investment account, and click Next twice.

11 If you entered a financial institution name in step 3, click the I Have No Other Accounts At This Institution option button.

12 Click Finish.

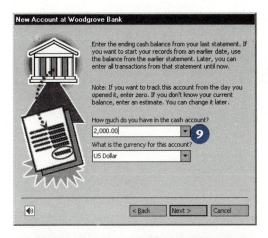

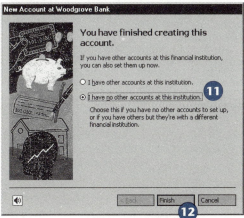

Describing Your Portfolio

Once you've set up your investment account, you're ready to describe the investments in your portfolio. You need to create these individual investments so that you can work with them later.

TIP

It's usually a good idea to enter each investment lot separately if you purchased different lots at different prices. If you don't want to go to this much work, however, you can just enter all the lots together as one big lot and use the average price you paid.

Describe Your Current Portfolio

1 Display the investment account's register.

2 Click New.

3 Enter the date you first purchased the investment.

4 Enter a name for the investment.

5 Click Enter to display the Create New Investment dialog box.

6 Select the option that most closely describes the investment you're adding, and click Next.

7 Use the fields that Money provides to describe the investment in more detail, and click Finish.

8 Click the down arrow in the Activity field, and select Buy from the list.

9 Enter the number of shares you own.

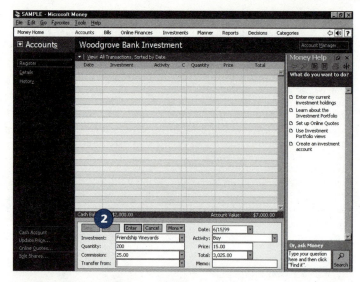

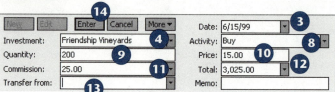

10 Enter the cost per unit you paid.

11 Enter any sales commission you paid.

12 Review the contents of the Total field, and edit the value if necessary.

13 Delete the account name shown in the Transfer From field. You don't want to reduce the cash balance for this transaction if it's an old investment purchase.

14 Click Enter to record the investment.

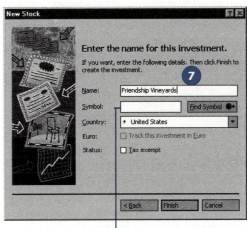

If you plan to use Money's Online Quotes feature, enter the security symbol.

The Portfolio Window

Once you've set up your investment accounts, described your investments, and updated their prices, you can use the Portfolio window to monitor your investments. To display the Portfolio window, click Investments on the navigation bar.

This view shows gain and return figures for your investments.

This view displays the latest quotes for your investments.

This view charts the distribution of funds by investment type.

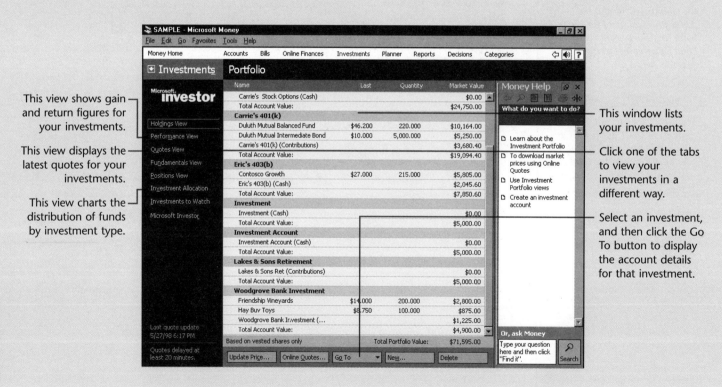

This window lists your investments.

Click one of the tabs to view your investments in a different way.

Select an investment, and then click the Go To button to display the account details for that investment.

Updating Prices

After you've described all the investments in your portfolio, you're ready to enter current price information. You'll want to do this so your investment records reflect current market values.

TIP

If you enter an incorrect price, select the price from the Update Price dialog box's list box, and then click Delete.

Update the Prices in Your Portfolio

1. Display the investment account register.

2. Click Update Price on the Accounts bar.

3. Click the down arrow in the Investment field, and select the investment whose current market price you want to update.

4. Enter the current date.

5. Enter the current market price.

6. Click Update.

7. Repeat steps 3 through 6 for the other investments you're holding.

8. Click Close.

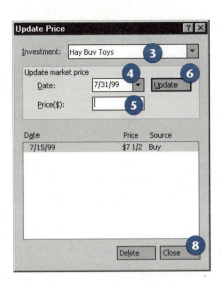

8

Using Online Quotes

With Money's Online Quotes service, you can download the latest prices of a stock or major mutual fund and, in so doing, automatically update your investment portfolio. The service costs $2.95 per month for six sessions. Additional downloads cost $.50 each. If you track a lot of stocks, you'll find that this service can save you time searching through the newspaper. Another advantage of the Online Quotes service for serious investors is that stock prices are updated every 15 minutes.

TIP

If you want to track stocks you don't actually own, click New in the Portfolio window and click the A New Investment option button.

Enter Market Symbols for Stocks and Mutual Funds

1 Click Investments on the navigation bar.

2 Click Quotes View on the Investments bar.

3 Select the investment, and click the Go To button.

4 Select Go To Details.

5 Enter the symbol or click Find Symbol to use Microsoft Investor to find the symbol.

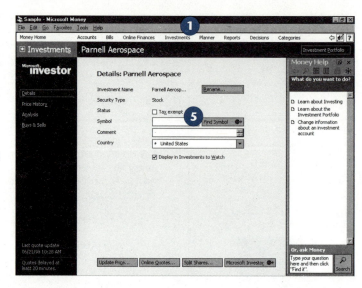

TIP

If you don't have an account with an Internet service provider, select Subscription Quotes and sign up for the service by filling out the application Money provides.

Download Market Prices

1 Click Investments on the navigation bar.

2 Click the Online Quotes button.

3 If you have never used Online Quotes before, select an Online Quotes service from the drop-down list box and click Next.

4 Select the country you're calling from and click Next.

5 Review the investments for which you've entered market-approved symbols. If you don't want to up-date one or more of the investments, clear the check box.

6 Click the Call button. You'll see a series of messages as your computer sends and receives information.

7 Click Close.

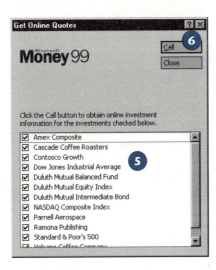

Recording Investment Purchases

After you've set up your investment accounts and described your current portfolio, you're ready to begin using Money for day-to-day record-keeping. Whenever you purchase more shares of a stock or mutual fund or additional bonds, you describe the purchase in the investment account's Account Register window.

TIP

If you haven't purchased the stock, bond, or mutual fund before, when you enter the name in the Investment field, Money displays the Create New Investment dialog box where you can set up the investment.

TIP

To describe a purchase or sale, you need to enter at least three of the following four inputs: Quantity, Price, Commission, and Total. If you leave one of these inputs blank, Money uses the other three inputs to calculate the fourth.

Record a Purchase

1. Display the investment account register.

2. Click New.

3. Enter the purchase date.

4. Enter a name for the investment, or select it from the list.

5. Click the down arrow in the Activity field, and select Buy from the list.

6. Indicate the number of stock or mutual fund shares or the number of individual bonds you're purchasing.

7. Enter the dollar price per share or the price per bond.

8. Record any sales commission you paid.

9. Verify the contents of the Total field, and edit the value, if necessary, to correctly reflect the total purchase price.

10. Click the down arrow in the Transfer From field, and select the bank account or associated cash account you are using to pay for the purchase.

11. Click Enter.

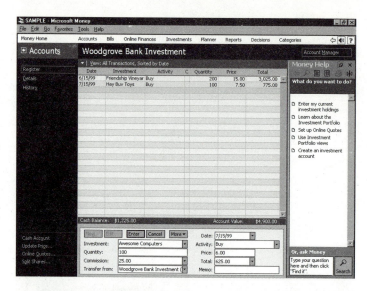

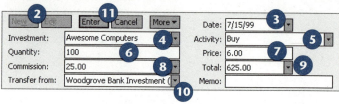

Building an Investment Watch List

With Money 99 Financial Suite, you can also monitor stocks you don't actually own. To do so, you use the Investments To Watch area of the Investments center.

SEE ALSO

See "Using Online Quotes" on pages 118–119 for information on downloading current stock prices.

Add an Investment to Watch

1. Click Investments on the navigation bar.

2. Click Investments To Watch on the Investments bar.

3. Click the Add button.

4. Click the Investment option button and click Next.

5. Select the type of investment you want to track and click Next.

6. Enter the name of the investment you want to track.

7. Enter the investment's symbol

8. Enter the country of the stock exchange on which the investment is found.

9. Click Finish.

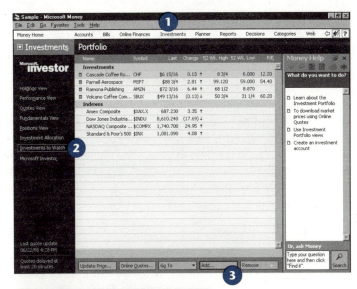

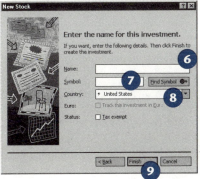

8

Recording Investment Sales

When you record the sale of an investment, you describe the transaction by following a series of steps similar to the steps you follow to purchase an investment.

Record a Sale

1 Display the investment account's register.

2 Click New.

3 Enter the sale date.

4 Click the down arrow in the Investment field, and select the name of the stock, bond, or mutual fund you're selling.

5 Click the down arrow in the Activity field, and select Sell from the list.

6 Enter the number of stock or mutual fund shares or the number of individual bonds you're selling.

7 Enter the price per share or price per bond you're receiving.

8 Record the commission you paid to sell the stock, bond, or mutual fund.

9 Verify the contents of the Total field, and edit the value if necessary, to reflect the total purchase amount.

10 Click the down arrow in the Transfer To field, and select the bank account or associated cash account in which you'll deposit the sale proceeds.

11 Click Enter.

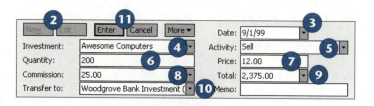

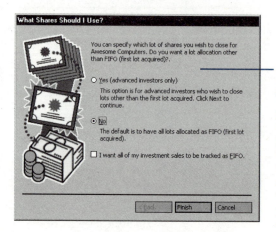

If you have more than one lot, Money asks if you want to specify the lot you want to sell. If you indicate that you want to sell a lot other than the first one you bought, click Next to specify the lot.

Recording Dividends and Distributions

Periodically, of course, you'll receive a mutual fund dividend distribution. Many stocks also pay dividends that you will have to record as well.

Record Dividends

1. Display the investment account's register.

2. Click New.

3. Enter the dividend date.

4. Click the down arrow in the Investment field, and select the name of the stock or mutual fund that is distributing the dividend.

5. Click the down arrow in the Activity field, and select an entry from the list. For dividends from stocks, select Dividend.

6. Specify the amount of the dividend.

7. Click the down arrow in the Transfer To field, and select the bank account or associated cash account in which you'll deposit the dividend.

8. Click Enter.

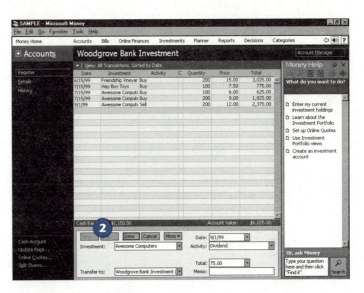

Reinvesting Dividends and Distributions

With a mutual fund, you usually have the option of reinvesting the distributions you receive when the mutual fund returns a profit. By reinvesting, you continue to accumulate more and more shares. Typically, reinvested distributions aren't subject to the same sales commissions that regular purchases are. Some stock companies also offer shareholders the opportunity to buy more shares with their dividends. As with mutual funds, these dividend reinvestment programs, often called DRIPs, let investors add to their holdings at a low cost because they typically don't require a brokerage commission.

TRY THIS

Fill out only the Price and Total fields, and Money calculates the quantity of shares.

Reinvest Dividends or Distributions

1 Display the investment account register.

2 Click New.

3 Enter the reinvestment date.

4 Click the down arrow in the Investment field, and select the name of the investment.

5 Click the down arrow in the Activity field, and select an appropriate entry to describe the reinvestment. Select Reinvest Dividend for dividends from stocks.

6 Describe how many mutual fund shares you're purchasing by reinvesting the distribution.

7 Give the price per share you're paying for the new mutual fund shares.

8 Record any commission you paid to purchase the investment.

9 Verify the contents of the Total field, and edit the value, if necessary, so that it correctly reflects the total purchase amount.

10 Click Enter.

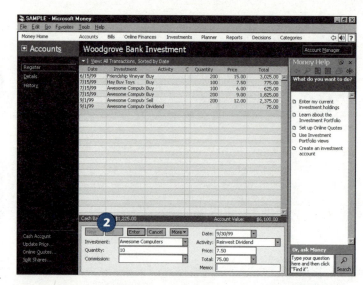

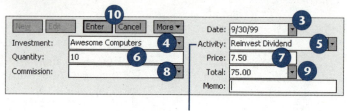

Select Reinvest Interest for a reinvested interest distribution, select Reinvest Dividend for a reinvested dividend distribution, select Reinvest S-Term CG Dist for a reinvested short-term capital gains distribution, or select Reinvest L-Term CG Dist for a reinvested long-term capital gains distribution.

Recording Other Income and Expenses

Money lets you record other income and expenses that don't fit into named categories. For example, if you have income that can't correctly be categorized as interest, dividends, or capital gains, you use the Other Income category. If you have an investment expense such as a brokerage account fee that you pay to maintain an account, use the Other Expense category.

TIP

If the income or expense amount is related only to the brokerage account in general, for example, and not to a specific investment, leave the Investment box empty.

TIP

If you buy stocks or bonds on margin, you record margin interest—the interest costs that your broker charges you on the borrowed money—as an Other Expense transaction.

Record Other Income or Expenses

1. Display the investment account register.

2. Click New.

3. Enter the transaction date.

4. Click the down arrow in the Investment field, and select the name of the investment.

5. Click the down arrow in the Activity field, and select either Other Income or Other Expense.

6. Categorize the income or expense amount in the same way you would for a bank account transaction.

7. Enter the income or expense amount.

8. Click the down arrow in the Transfer From or Transfer To field, and select the account into which you'll deposit the income or from which you'll pay the expense.

9. Click Enter.

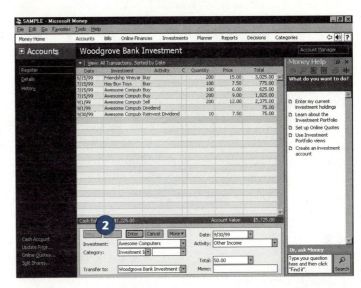

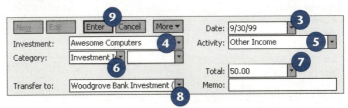

Recording Stock Splits

Companies whose share prices are growing quickly sometimes split shares of their stock to reduce the price per share, thereby making it easier for investors to buy even, one-hundred-share lots of the stock.

TIP

Stock dividends. *A stock dividend is a dividend that is paid in stock. As a practical matter, however, a stock dividend works exactly like a stock split. For example, if a stock pays a dividend equal to one-twentieth of a share, you get 21 new shares for every 20 old ones. Because the market is smart enough to adjust accordingly, this is the same as a 21:20 split.*

Record a Stock Split

1. Display the investment account register.

2. Click Split Shares on the Accounts bar.

3. Click the down arrow in the Investment field, and select the stock that's splitting.

4. Enter the stock split date.

5. Enter the number of new shares you're receiving.

6. Enter the number of old shares you had before the split.

7. Click OK.

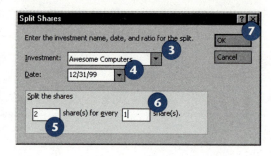

Recording Bond Interest

Bonds typically reward their holders by regularly paying interest. You record interest in the same way you record dividends and distributions for stocks and mutual funds.

> **TIP**
>
> *Some bonds, such as zero-coupon bonds, don't pay interest over the course of their life. Instead, these bonds pay interest at the very end, when the bond is redeemed. See "Accrued Interest on Bonds" on page 130 for more information about how to treat zero-coupon bonds.*

> **TIP**
>
> **Return of capital.** *A return of capital is the return of a portion of the price you originally paid. To record a return of capital, or a liquidated dividend, select Return Of Capital from the Activity field. You know that a dividend is a return of capital because the statement you receive with the payment will identify it as such.*

Record Bond Interest

1. Display the investment account register.

2. Click New.

3. Enter the interest payment date.

4. Click the down arrow in the Investment field, and select the name of the bond paying the interest.

5. Click the down arrow in the Activity field, and select Interest.

6. Enter the amount of the interest payment.

7. Click the down arrow in the Transfer To field, and select the bank account or associated cash account in which you'll deposit the interest payment.

8. Click Enter.

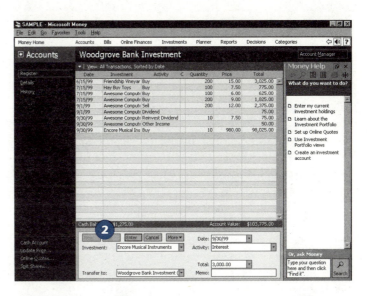

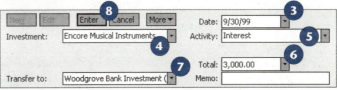

Bond Premiums and Bond Discounts

If you pay more for a bond than the redemption price, the extra amount you pay is called a *premium*. You might ask, why would you and other investors pay more for a bond than the borrower will pay to redeem it? Because the borrower agrees to pay a higher rate of interest than the current rate. For example, imagine that a borrower issues $1,000 bonds that pay 6.6 percent interest, or $66. Subsequent to the issue of the bonds, investors like you decide that 6 percent is the going bond interest rate; a bond that pays $66 is therefore worth more than $1,000 because $66 is 6 percent of $1,100, not $1,000.

Bond premiums present an accounting problem. In effect, the $100 is an expense, or loss. Why? Although you might pay $1,100 for the bond described in the preceding paragraph, you only receive $1,000 when you redeem it.

For record-keeping purposes, you should spread the expense of the $100 bond premium over the years until the borrower redeems the bond. This is called amortization. To amortize the bond premium, multiply the effective interest rate the bond earns by its purchase price, and then subtract this amount from the actual interest the bond pays during the year. The difference is the bond premium expense that you will record the first year.

In the years that follow, you make only one minor modification in this bond-premium allocation formula.

Instead of multiplying the effective interest rate the bond earns by the bond purchase price, you multiply the effective interest rate by the bond purchase price minus the bond premium amounts that you've already allocated.

Suppose, for example, that you purchase a $1,050 bond that pays an effective interest rate, or yield to maturity, of 6 percent. Further suppose that the bond pays $66 in interest annually. Given these facts, the bond premium charged as expense the first year would be calculated like this:

$$\$66 - (6\% \times \$1,050) = \$3$$

During the second year, the bond premium that is charged as an expense would be calculated as follows:

$$\$66 - [6\% \times (\$1,050 - \$3)] = \$3.18$$

During the third year, the bond premium charged as an expense would be calculated like so:

$$\$66 - [6\% \times (\$1,050 - \$3 - \$3.18)] = \$3.56$$

To record the allocations of bond premiums as expenses, you record two transactions. Record the bond premium allocation as an Other Expense for the bond, and specify the Transfer From account as the associated cash account. Record a return of capital transaction equal to the bond premium allocation, and specify the Transfer To account as the associated cash account.

Handling Bond Discounts

Bond discounts arise when buyers pay less for a bond than its redemption price. The difference between the purchase price and the redemption price is called the *discount*. A discount indicates that the borrower is paying less than the current rate.

Accounting for bond discounts works much like accounting for bond premiums. Suppose, for example, that a borrower issues a $1,000 bond that pays 6 percent interest, or $60, and that subsequent to the issue, investors decide that 6.66 percent should be the going rate. In this case, a bond that pays $60 is worth less than $1,000, because $60 is 6.66 percent of $900, not $1,000.

The $100 difference is income because, although you might pay $900 for the bond described in the preceding paragraph, you'll receive $1,000 when you redeem it. You should treat the $100 bond discount you receive as income and spread it over the years between the purchase and the redemption.

To make this discount allocation, you multiply the effective interest rate the bond earns by the bond purchase price and then subtract from this figure the actual interest the bond paid for the year. The difference is the bond discount income you record for the year. The effective interest rate is simply the yield to maturity—a figure you'll obtain when you purchase the bond.

In following years, you modify this bond-discount allocation formula by multiplying the effective interest rate by the bond purchase price plus the bond discount amounts already allocated.

Suppose that you purchase a $950 bond that pays an effective interest rate of 6.5 percent. This bond annually pays $60 in interest. Given these facts, the bond discount allocated as income the first year would be calculated like this:

$$(6.5\% \times \$950) - \$60 = \$1.75$$

During the second year, the bond discount allocated as income would be calculated as follows:

$$[6.5\% \times (\$950 + \$1.75)] - \$60 = \$1.86$$

During the third year, the bond discount allocated as income would be calculated like so:

$$[6.5\% \times (\$950 + \$1.75 + \$1.86)] - \$60 = \$1.98$$

To record the allocations of bond discounts as income, you treat the bond discount as accrued interest—which, in fact, is what it is. To do this, you first record the accrued bond interest (the bond discount allocation) as regular interest income. When you record this transaction, transfer the bond interest income to your associated cash account, even though there really won't be a deposit. (The interest will only accrue.) Then record a negative return of capital transaction equal to the accrued interest. When you record this second transaction, transfer the bond interest income out of your associated cash account. This way, Money records the interest income and adjusts the bond value for the accrued interest.

8

Accrued Interest on Bonds

Unless you buy or sell a bond on the interest payment day, some of what you pay when you buy the bond and some of what you receive when you sell it represents accrued interest. Accrued interest is simply the interest the bond has earned since the last interest payment date. Unfortunately, accrued interest increases both the work and the complexity of bond record-keeping.

Accrued Interest on Bonds You Purchase

To record the purchase of a bond with accrued interest, you record two transactions. For example, let's say you just purchased, for $1,020, a $1,000 bond with $20 of accrued interest. First, record the purchase of the actual bond without the accrued interest: $1,000. Then, record a return of capital transaction with a negative return of capital amount equal to the accrued interest (in this case, $20). At this point, Money shows your bond's value as equal to $1,020.

When you get your next interest payment—let's say it's $60—you record two transactions: a return of capital transaction equal to $20 and an interest income transaction equal to $40. In this way, you don't count

as income the $20 of accrued interest you actually paid when you purchased the bond. And you record as interest income only the $40 you actually earned.

Accrued Interest on Bonds You Own

Some bonds accrue interest but don't pay the interest. (The bond issuer typically reports this accrued but unpaid interest on form 1099-OID at the end of the year.) To keep a good record of these bonds, you need to record the accrued interest annually because the interest income is taxable. To do this, you record two transactions. First, you record the accrued bond interest as regular interest income. When you record this transaction, transfer the bond interest income to your associated cash account—even though there really won't be a deposit because the interest will only accrue. Then record a negative return of capital transaction equal to the accrued interest. When you record this second transaction, transfer the bond interest income from your associated cash account. In this way, Money records the interest income and adjusts the bond value for the accrued interest.

Real Estate Investing

Many investors prize real estate because it is a hedge against inflation and because many types of real estate investments deliver solid cash returns. Real estate investments present unusual record-keeping challenges, however, both for passive real estate investors and for active real estate investors.

Passive real estate investors put their money into real estate investments they don't actively manage such as limited partnership units or shares and real estate investment trusts, or REITs. While that sounds straightforward, recording the income and expenses of passive real estate investments is unfortunately more complicated than, say, recording the income and expenses that pertain to stocks or bonds. (Don't worry if you don't understand this lingo yet—I'll go into more detail in a minute.)

Active real estate investors actually buy, sell, and manage their real estate investments, treating their investments as, essentially, a business. Not surprisingly, then, active real estate investments require you to set up business bookkeeping systems. Despite these challenges, Microsoft Money provides real estate investors with a wonderful set of tools and possibilities.

Creating Passive Real Estate Investment Accounts

Passive real estate investments include limited partnership units and shares in real estate investment trusts. At first glance, these investments resemble stocks, but they actually work quite differently because not all the cash you receive comes in the form of interest or dividends. Typically, a substantial portion of the distributions from a passive real estate investment represents a return of capital. Despite their complexity, however, you can use Money to keep accurate financial records of passive real estate investments.

Lakes & Sons REIT

Set Up a Passive Real Estate Investment Account

1 Click Accounts on the navigation bar once or twice to display the Account Manager window.

2 Click the New Account button.

3 Optionally, enter the name of the financial institution associated with the account, and click Next.

4 Select Investment from the list of accounts, and click Next.

5 Enter a name for the investment account, and click Next.

6 Specify whether the account is tax deferred by selecting the appropriate option, and click Next.

7 Enter the estimated value of the real estate investments in the account.

8 Specify whether the account has an associated cash account, and click Next.

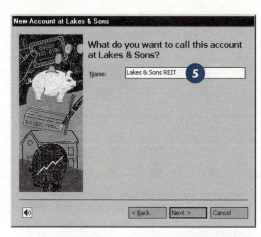

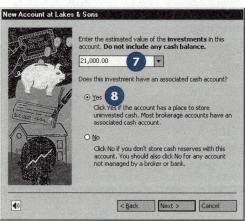

The best way to start investing in real estate. *Invest in your own home. On average, home ownership investment has delivered returns roughly equal to those of the stock market. Note, however, that it's difficult to make money on any real estate investment—including the purchase of a home—unless you hold the investment for a lengthy period of time. Typically, you need several years of appreciation just to pay for the selling costs.*

9 If the account does have an associated cash account, enter the cash account's ending balance from your last monthly statement, and click Next.

10 If a financial institution is associated with the account, Money asks if you have any other accounts to set up. Click the I Have No Other Accounts At This Institution option button, and click Next.

11 Click Finish.

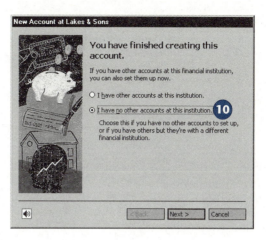

New Account at Lakes & Sons

You have finished creating this account.

If you have other accounts at this financial institution, you can also set them up now.

○ I have other accounts at this institution.

● I have no other accounts at this institution. **10**

Choose this if you have no other accounts to set up, or if you have others but they're with a different financial institution.

< Back   Next >   Cancel

9

Recording Real Estate Investment Purchases

Whenever you purchase partnership units or shares in a real estate investment trust, you need to describe the purchase in the investment account's Account Register window. The process of recording a passive real estate investment purchase is the same as the process for recording a stock, bond, or mutual fund purchase.

House

Record a Passive Real Estate Investment Purchase

1. Display the investment account register.

2. Click New.

3. Enter the purchase date.

4. Enter a name for the investment. If you haven't purchased units or shares of the real estate partnership or investment trust before, Money displays the Create New Investment dialog box.

5. Click the Stock option button, click Next, and then click Finish.

6. Click the down arrow in the Activity field, and select Buy from the list.

7. Enter the number of partnership units or trust shares you're purchasing.

8. Enter the price per unit or share you're paying.

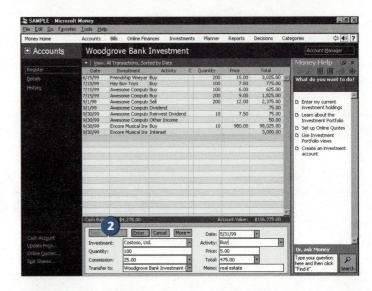

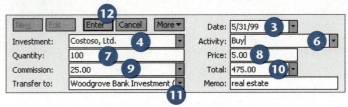

Passive real estate investments. *In a passive real estate investment, you don't actively manage the investment. For example, you don't pick a property manager, collect rent, or arrange financing. If you purchased shares of a real estate investment trust (REIT) or invested in a real estate project as a limited partner, your investment is probably passive.*

If you're describing a publicly traded real estate investment and you intend to use Money's Online Quotes feature, you need to enter the security symbol in the Create New Investment dialog box. Refer to "Using Online Quotes" on pages 118–119.

9 Record any sales commission you paid.

10 Verify the contents of the Total field, and edit the value, if necessary, so that it correctly reflects the total purchase amount.

11 Click the down arrow in the Transfer From field, and select the bank account or associated cash account you're using to purchase the investment. Keep this box blank if you're recording a past purchase.

12 Click Enter.

Create New Investment

What type of investment is it?

○ Mutual Fund (including those that invest in stocks, bonds and/or index fund)

⦿ Stock (common, preferred, and options) **5**

○ CD (Certificate of Deposit)

○ Money Market

○ Bond (Interest-paying bonds, including T-Notes, T-Bonds)

○ Discounted Bond (Zero-coupon bonds, including T-Bills, Savings Bonds)

○ Employee Stock Option Grant

[Next >] [Cancel]

9

Recording Real Estate Investment Sales

When you sell units or shares of a real estate invest-ment, of course, you de-scribe that transaction too. You record the sale of a real estate investment in the same way that you record the sale of a stock or mutual fund shares or individual bonds.

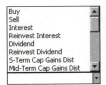

TIP

If you sell only a portion of a specific real estate investment and you own more than one lot, Money gives you the option of specifying which lot you're selling.

Record a Real Estate Investment Sale

1 Display the investment account register, and click New.

2 Enter the sale date.

3 Identify the name of the real estate investment you're selling.

4 Click the down arrow in the Activity field, and se-lect Sell from the list.

5 Describe how many part-nership units or trust shares you're selling.

6 Enter the price per share or per unit you're receiv-ing.

7 Record any sales commis-sion you paid to sell the units or shares.

8 Verify the contents of the Total field, and edit the value, if necessary, to cor-rectly reflect the total pur-chase amount.

9 Click the down arrow in the Transfer To field, and select the bank account or associated cash account in which you'll deposit the sale proceeds.

10 Click Enter.

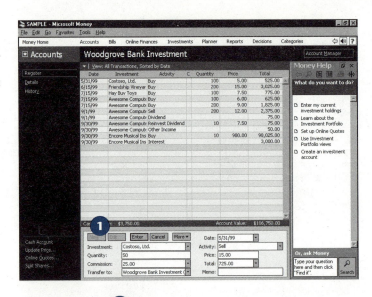

Recording Real Estate Investment Distributions

At the end of the quarter or the end of the year, you usually receive a real estate investment fund dividend distribution, which you then need to record.

TIP

Select Interest for an interest distribution, Dividend for a dividend distribution, S-Term Cap Gains Dist for a short-term capital gains distribution, L-Term Cap Gains for a long-term capital gains distribution, or Other Income.

TIP

The quarterly or year-end distribution statement you receive identifies the type of distribution. You don't have to worry about making this determination.

Record a Real Estate Investment Distribution

1. Display the investment account register and click New.

2. Enter the distribution date.

3. Click the down arrow in the Investment field, and select the investment fund making the distribution.

4. Click the down arrow in the Activity field, and select an entry from the list.

5. Specify the amount of the distribution.

6. Click the down arrow in the Transfer To field, and select the bank account or associated cash account in which you'll deposit the distribution.

7. Click Enter to record the distribution.

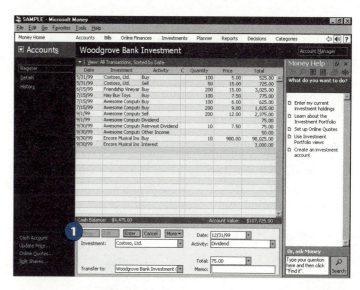

Recording Return of Capital Transactions

Sometimes a distribution isn't a share of the real estate profits but a return of capital—a return of a portion of the price you originally paid. Recording a return of capital for real estate investments works the same way as it does for stocks and bonds.

Record a Return of Capital Transaction

1. Display the investment account register.

2. Click New.

3. Enter the return of capital date.

4. Click the down arrow in the Investment field, and select the investment.

5. Click the down arrow in the Activity field, and select Return Of Capital from the list.

6. Enter the amount of the capital return.

7. Click the down arrow in the Transfer To field, and select the bank account or associated cash account in which you'll deposit the return of capital.

8. Click Enter.

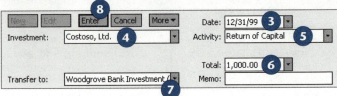

Setting Up Real Estate Property Accounts

If you're an active real estate investor, you can also use Money to simplify and expedite your record-keeping. In essence, you'll use Money to track three things: the adjusted cost basis of your properties, the mortgages associated with any of your properties, and the income and expenses that individual properties produce. To track the adjusted cost basis of your investments, you must first set up asset accounts for each individual property you own.

5387 242nd Place

SEE ALSO

For information about making mortgage refinancing decisions, see "When to Repay and Refinance Mortgages" on pages 108–109.

Set Up an Active Real Estate Investment Account

1 Click Accounts on the navigation bar once or twice to display the Account Manager window.

2 Click the New Account button.

3 Leave the Bank or Financial Institution field empty, and click Next.

4 Select Asset from the list of accounts, and click Next.

5 Enter a name for the asset account, and the date you set up the account and click Next.

6 Enter the original purchase price of the property.

7 Money asks whether a loan is associated with the investment. Select the appropriate option.

8 If there is a loan associated with the investment, click Next and enter the name of the loan account.

9 Click Finish.

9

Building a Real Estate Investment Category List

To keep records of an individual property's income and expenses, you do two very simple things. First you create a list of categories specifically for tracking your real estate investments. Next you use these real estate income and expense categories to record transactions related to your real estate investments.

TIP

Although you can use any list of income or expense categories you want, you should base your categories on Schedule E of the federal income tax form, which you use to report your real estate profits or losses to the federal government.

Add a Real Estate Income or Expense Category

1. Click Categories on the navigation bar.

2. Click the New button.

3. Click the Create A New Category option button, and click Next.

4. Enter a name for the new real estate category.

5. Specify whether the new category is an income or expense category by selecting the appropriate option, and then click Next.

6. Select a general group to describe the new category from the list, and click Finish.

7. Repeat steps 2 through 6 to add each of the income and expense categories you need.

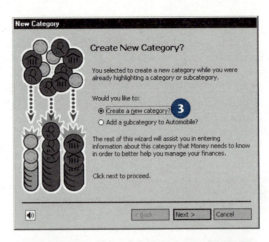

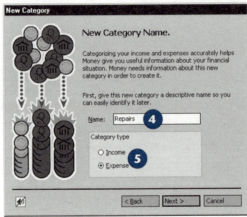

Setting Up Property Classifications

If you own more than one piece of property, you'll also want to create classifications to track each property's income and expenses. To create property classifications, you need to first turn on the classification feature, and then you need to create a classification for each property you own.

TIP

Once you create a Properties classification, the Properties field shows up in the transaction forms for all your asset, bank, and cash accounts.

TRY THIS

You may want to use a property's street address as its classification name.

Turn on the Classification Feature

1. Click Categories on the navigation bar.

2. Click the Classification 1 tab. Money displays the Add Classification dialog box.

3. Click the Properties option button.

4. Click OK.

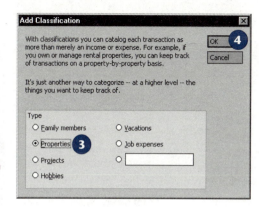

Create Property Classifications

1. Click Categories on the navigation bar.

2. Click the Properties tab.

3. Click the New button.

4. Enter the name of the real estate investment.

5. Click OK.

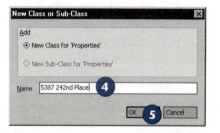

9

Tracking the Adjusted Cost of Property

Once you set up an asset account, you can use it to track improvements you make to the property (because improvements increase the property's adjusted cost) and your annual depreciation (because depreciation decreases the property's adjusted cost). The adjusted cost basis of a property is important. When you some day sell the property, you calculate the capital gain or loss by subtracting the adjusted cost from the net sales price.

TIP

Depreciation. *The tax laws treat various types of property differently when it comes to depreciation. How you depreciate a real estate property also depends on the tax laws in effect the year you placed the property into service. If you need help, consult a tax advisor or contact the Internal Revenue Service.*

Record Depreciation

1. Display the real estate property's asset account register.

2. Click the Decrease tab, and if necessary, click New.

3. Enter the date for the asset depreciation transaction.

4. Optionally, enter a description of the asset depreciation in the Pay To field.

5. Enter the amount of the annual depreciation charge.

6. Enter Depreciation in the Category field. If you have not recorded depreciation before, Money displays the New Category dialog box. Enter a description of the category, and click Enter.

7. Classify the real estate investment in the Properties field.

8. Click Enter.

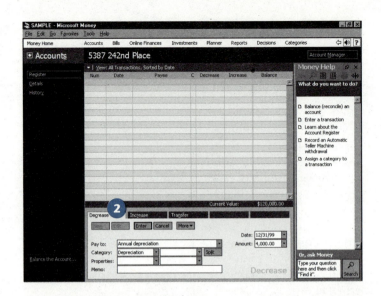

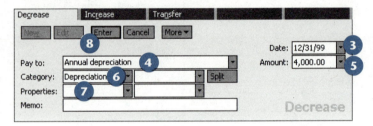

TIP

If you're entering a series of annual depreciation transactions, use a different year in the Date field for each transaction so that they get counted in a different year's profit or loss calculation.

TIP

Capital improvement vs. repairs and maintenance.

When you spend money fixing up a real estate property, you need to determine whether the expenditure is a capital improvement or a repairs and maintenance expense. You add capital improvement expenditures to the property's asset account, thereby increasing the adjusted cost. You use repairs and maintenance expenditures only to calculate the current year's profit or loss. It typically makes more sense to call an expenditure a repairs and maintenance expense than it does to call it a capital improvement. You can't make this decision yourself, however. The IRS has specific guidelines about what does and doesn't constitute a capital improvement. The general rule, however, is that if an expenditure adds to a property's useful life or its functionality, it's a capital improvement.

Record a Capital Improvement

1. Display the register for the bank account or associated cash account you'll use to pay for the capital improvements.

2. Click the Check tab, and if necessary, click New.

3. Enter the check number.

4. Enter the check date.

5. Enter the name of the person or business you're paying.

6. Enter the check amount.

7. Click the down arrow in the Category field, and select Transfer from the list.

8. Click the down arrow in the Subcategory field, and select the name of the property account.

9. Classify the real estate investment in the Properties field.

10. Enter a memo describing the improvement in detail.

11. Click Enter.

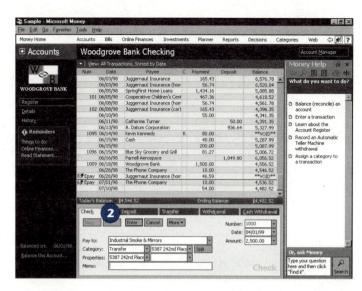

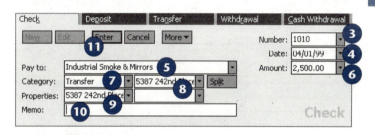

Recording Real Estate Income and Expense Transactions

After you've created a list of income and expense categories, keep your checkbook as usual—except when you record an income or expense related to a real estate property. Then you use the appropriate real estate income or expense category and describe the real estate investment using the Properties fields.

Record Real Estate Income

1. Display the register for the bank account or associated cash account in which you want to deposit the real estate income.

2. Click the Deposit tab, and if necessary, click New.

3. Enter the check number.

4. Enter the deposit date.

5. Enter the name of the person or business who paid you.

6. Enter the amount of the check.

7. Click the down arrow in the Category field, and select a real estate income category that describes the deposit.

8. Click the down arrow in the Properties field, and select the real estate property's classification.

9. Click Enter.

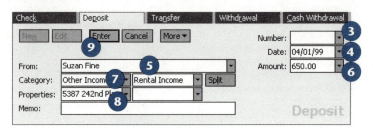

SEE ALSO

For more information on using bank accounts, see Section 3.

Record Real Estate Expense

1 Display the register for the bank account or associated cash account from which you want to pay for the real estate expense.

2 Click the Check tab, and if necessary, click New.

3 Enter the check number.

4 Enter the date.

5 Enter the name of the person or business you're paying.

6 Enter the amount of the check.

7 Click the down arrow in the Category field, and select a real estate expense category that describes the expenditure.

8 Click the down arrow in the Properties field, and select the real estate property's classification.

9 Click Enter.

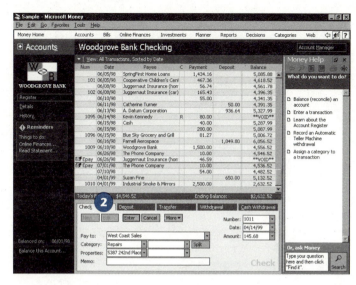

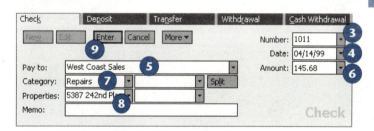

9

Reporting on Active Real Estate Investments

Once you collect income and expense data for active real estate investments, it is easy to create a report that summarizes income and expense data by property.

TRY THIS

Use this Income vs. Spending report to get most of the data you need to complete the Schedule E form.

Produce a Real Estate Investment Report

1 Click Reports on the navigation bar.

2 Click the Spending Habits button.

3 Select Income vs. Spending from the Spending Habits list.

4 Click the Go To Report/Chart button.

5 Click the Customize button to display the Customize Report dialog box.

6 Click the down arrow in the Columns field, and select Properties from the list.

7 Click OK to update the Income vs. Spending report using different columns to show income and spending by real estate investment.

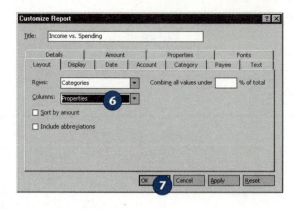

Choosing Appropriate Real Estate Investment Categories

The following figure shows the standard income and expense categories from the 1997 Schedule E used to report supplemental income from rental real estate. These categories can change from year to year. If you can't get a newer form, however, this outdated form is a good one to base your categories in Money on because you need to begin tracking income and expenses at the start of the year, before the new Schedule E form for the current year comes out. Although you can't be certain that the categories you use in Money will match the form you'll have to use, you'll probably not be far off.

9

Income:		Properties			Totals (Add columns A, B, and C.)	
		A	B	C		
3 Rents received	3				3	
4 Royalties received	4				4	
Expenses:						
5 Advertising	5					
6 Auto and travel (see page E-2)	6					
7 Cleaning and maintenance	7					
8 Commissions	8					
9 Insurance	9					
10 Legal and other professional fees	10					
11 Management fees	11					
12 Mortgage interest paid to banks, etc. (see page E-2)	12				12	
13 Other interest	13					
14 Repairs	14					
15 Supplies	15					
16 Taxes	16					
17 Utilities	17					
18 Other (list) ▶						
	18					

Online Banking, Bill Payment, and Web Browsing

One way to take advantage of the power of emerging online technologies is by using any or all of Microsoft Money's online features:

◆ Online Bill Payment

◆ Online Banking

◆ Integrated Web Browsing with Microsoft Internet Explorer

You might have read an article or two about home banking and how it will revolutionize the way people interact with their banks. More and more banks now offer some sort of online services. Users of version 3 of Microsoft Money had only three banks in the entire country to choose from if they wanted to bank online. Now more than 100 banks participate, including some of the largest in the country.

You can use any or all of Money's online services. The services are tightly integrated into the program and require no additional software. To use all three of the services, however, you do need a modem. To browse the World Wide Web from within Money, you also need an Internet connection. And to use online banking, you need to hold an account at a participating bank.

Setting Up an Internet Connection

The integration of Internet Explorer and Money allows you to complete a wide array of online tasks directly from the Money program window. If you've never used Internet Explorer 4 before, you need to first set the program up to work with your modem and Internet service provider connection. You need to do this if you want to take advantage of any of Money's online features, even if you're not planning to bank or pay bills online.

TIP

To customize your connection settings in Money, choose the Tools menu's Options command and click the Connection tab. Use this tab's boxes and buttons to specify what you want Money to retrieve when you connect to the Internet, when you want to connect to the Internet, and which browser you want to use.

Sign Up For and Set Up an Account with an Internet Service Provider

1. Make sure you modem is plugged in, turned on, and connected to your phone line.

2. Choose the Tools menu's Connection Settings command.

3. Click Connect to start the Internet Connection Wizard.

4. Select the first option and click Next. The Internet Connection Wizard dials a toll-free number and then displays a list of Internet service providers in your area.

5. Select a service and click Next to sign up for an account. Fill out the personal information the Wizard requests, and click Next to display a Web page run by the Internet service provider.

6. Follow the ISP's instructions to continue applying for an account.

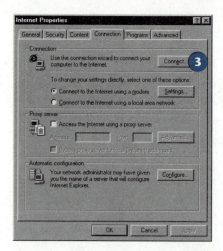

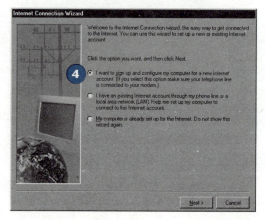

To update the headlines and information in your Financial Home Page and to update stock prices all at once, choose the Tools menu's Update Internet Information command.

Click the Yes option button in step 7 to change the phone number you want to dial, your account name, or your password.

Set Up an Existing Internet Connection

1 Choose the Tools menu's Connection Settings command.

2 Click Connect to start the Internet Connection Wizard.

3 Click the second option and click Next.

4 Tell Money whether you connect to the Internet over a local area network or an Internet service provider or whether you have an account with an online service, and click Next.

5 Specify the type of connection you chose and click Next.

6 Click the Use An Existing Dial-Up Connection option, select the connection you want to use, and click Next.

7 Click the No option button to retain your current connection settings. Then click Next.

8 Proceed through the Wizard to set up new Internet mail, news, and directory service accounts if necessary.

9 Click Finish.

10

Setting Up Online Services

Once you have a modem installed and working properly, you can set up online services in Money. With Online Banking, you can download your bank statements and transactions and transfer money between online accounts. With Online Bill Payment, you can send checks electronically.

Woodgrove Bank Checking

TIP

If you haven't yet created the account for which you want to use Money's online services, click the Create New Account button to create the account. See "Setting Up Bank Accounts" on page 16 for more information about creating bank accounts.

Set Up Online Banking and Bill Payment

1. Click Online Finances on the navigation bar.

2. Select the account to which you're interested in adding online functionality and click Go To.

3. Click Investigate Offerings to find out what online services your bank offers for Money users.

4. Click Next to connect with the Online Services Directory.

5. Click Financial Institutions to select the name of your bank from the list of banks that offer online services with Money.

6. Select your bank and click OK.

7. Make sure your modem is turned on and plugged in, and click Next to connect to the Internet and download information about your bank's online service offerings.

8. Click Finish.

9. Follow your bank's procedures for setting up online services for your account. You may be able to do

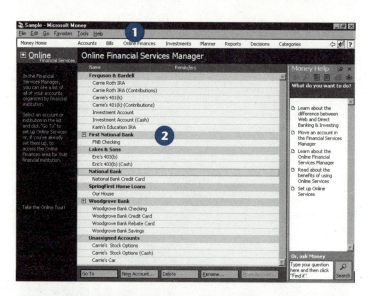

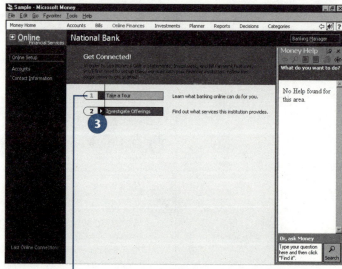

Click the Take A Tour button to learn more about what you can do with online services.

this online, or you may need to call your bank or go to the bank in person to apply and pick up all the information you need.

10 After you have all the information you need from your bank, click Set Up Online Services to begin setting up your Money accounts to use online banking.

11 Click Next to begin, then click Yes, I Have This Information, and click Next.

12 Enter the personal information Money requests, and click Next.

13 Click Next to accept the financial institution number Money provides.

14 Select the account that you want to use for online services, and click Next.

15 Check the boxes next to the services that you've set up for use with the account, and click Next.

16 Enter your account number, the account type, and your bank's routing number, and click Next.

17 Click Next if you have no other accounts to set up, and then click Finish.

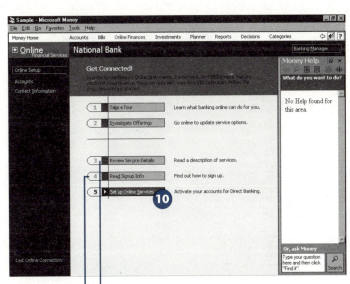

Click Review Service Details to read about which online services your bank offers.

Click Read Signup Info to find out how you can sign up for online services with your bank.

10

Downloading Bank Account Records

Before you can use online banking services, you must have an account set up at a participating bank. Then once you're set up, you can easily download statements from your bank, transfer money between accounts, and even order new checks. Downloading your statements is a cinch. It involves two steps: downloading the records and adding the downloaded transactions to your account register.

TIP

If your account is set up for Web banking, select the account in the Online Finances area and click Go To. Then click the Connect tab and click the Go To Web Site button. Web banking differs for each bank, so follow your bank's instructions.

Download Bank Account Records

1 Click Online Finances on the navigation bar.

2 Select the account whose statement you want to download and click Go To.

3 Click Connect on the Online bar.

4 Click the Connect button.

5 If this is the first time you're connecting to your bank, Money asks you to change your PIN number. Enter the online PIN number you received from your bank, and then enter a new PIN number in the fields provided. Click OK.

6 Optionally, click the Dialing Properties button to customize the way in which Microsoft Windows handles your calls.

7 Click the Connect button. You'll see a series of messages as your computer sends and then receives information.

8 Confirm that the call was completed successfully, and click Close.

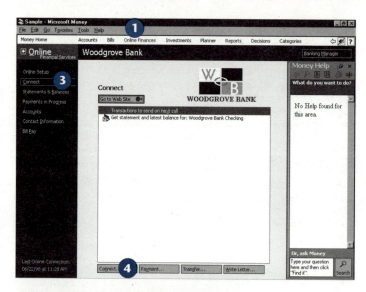

Add Downloaded Transactions to the Account Register

1 Click Statements & Balances on the Online bar.

2 Select an account from the list, and click the Read Statement button.

3 Click the Update Account Register button.

4 For each transaction, Money tries to find a matching transaction in your account register. When it finds one that appears to match, you then confirm whether this is the same transaction or ask Money to keep looking.

5 If Money doesn't find a match for a transaction, it displays the transaction and gives you a chance to make any changes. At this point, you might want to change the payee name or add a category or sub-category.

6 Make any changes you want to each downloaded transaction, and click Next to move on to the next one.

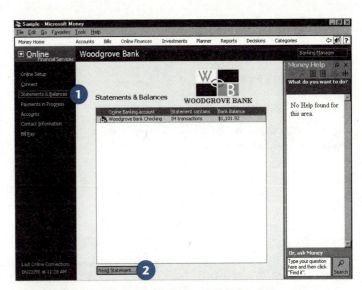

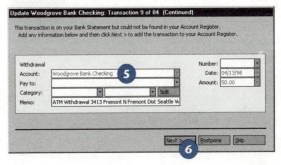

10

Making Electronic Payments

With Money's Online Bill Payment service, you can pay any business or individual in the United States right from your computer. The service works with any checking account in the United States, and the suggested retail price is $4.95 per month for 20 payments. Additional payments are usually about $.50 each.

TIP

If your account is set up for Web bill payment, select the account in the Online Finances area and click Go To. Then click the Connect tab and click the Go To Web Site button. Follow your bank's procedures for paying the bill, and then record the bill in Money as a regular check.

Enter an Electronic Payment

1 Display the register for the account you've set up for online services.

2 Click the Check tab, and click New, if necessary.

3 Click the down arrow in the Number field, and select Epay from the list.

4 Enter the date you want the payment delivered (or the payment's due date).

5 Enter the name of the payee. This name will appear on the envelope and the Pay To line of the check. If you've never made out a check to this payee, Money will display the Online Payee Details box, asking for the payee's contact information.

6 Make sure this is the way you want the payee's name to appear on the check and the envelope.

7 Enter the address, including the 5- or 9-digit zip code of the payee. Use the second line of the street address field, if necessary.

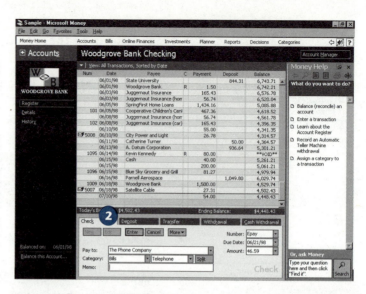

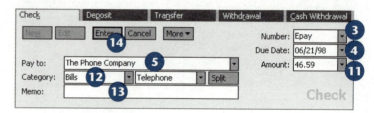

8 Optionally, enter the phone number of the payee. Although this is not required, it is a good idea in case there is a problem with the payment.

9 If the payment is going to a business with which you have an account, such as the phone company, enter your account number.

10 Click OK to return to the register.

11 Enter the amount of the payment.

12 Categorize the payment.

13 Enter a memo.

14 Click Enter.

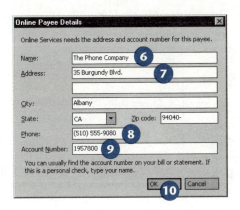

10

Sending Electronic Payments

Once you enter all your electronic payments, the next step is to send them to the online services. Then the check is cut so that it can be sent through the mail to the payee.

> ❶ **Reminder**
> You have 1 Electronic Payment to send.
>   ◆ Online Finances...

TRY THIS

If you have an electronic payment entered but not yet sent and you're in the account register, you can click Online Finances on the Accounts bar to go to Online Finances and send the payment.

TIP

Use the Dialing Properties dialog box to disable call waiting or to enter a number to access an outside line.

Send an Electronic Payment

1 Click Online Finances on the navigation bar.

2 Select the account from which you want to make the payment and click Go To.

3 Click Connect on the Online bar, and review the payment information you entered. If you subscribe to the Online Banking service, you'll also see instructions for updating the statement and balance of your Online Banking accounts.

4 Click the Connect button.

5 Enter your PIN number.

6 Optionally, click the Dialing Properties button to customize the way in which Windows handles your calls.

7 Click the Connect button to send the payment instructions. You'll see a progression of messages as your payment is sent and received.

8 Confirm that the transaction was completed successfully, and click Close.

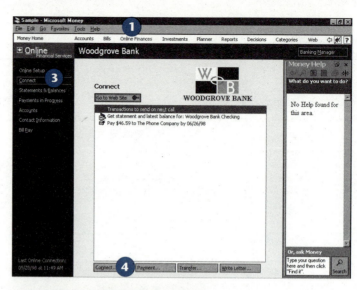

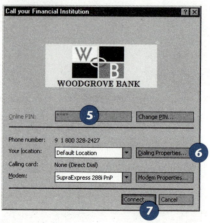

TIP

If you haven't yet sent the electronic payment (if it still says "Epay" next to the open envelope icon in the Number field of the account register), you can cancel it by selecting it and pressing the Delete key.

TIP

To see the status of an electronic payment you've made in the last 60 days, click Payments In Progress and then click the Payment Status button. Money displays the payment status, the date it was transmitted, and whether you marked the transaction as cleared.

Cancel an Electronic Payment

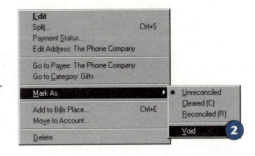

1. Display the account register with the electronic payment you want to cancel.

2. Right-click the transaction you want to cancel, and choose the shortcut menu's Mark As command and the Mark As submenu's Void command.

3. Click the Yes option button when Money asks whether you want to create an instruction to cancel the payment.

4. Click Online Finances on the navigation bar.

5. Select the account with the payment you want to cancel and click Go To.

6. Click Connect on the Online bar, and make sure the cancel payment instruction is there.

7. Click the Connect button to send the cancellation instruction to the bank.

Making Automatic Payments

If you want to take the convenience of online bill payment one step further, you can also tell the Online Bill Payment service to make payments for you automatically so that you don't have to remember to connect to your bank to send the payment instruction. This only works for recurring payments of a fixed amount, such as rent, car, and mortgage payments. When you authorize an automatic payment, the checks are sent weekly, monthly, bimonthly, or at whatever frequency you specify.

Create an Automatic Payment

1. Click Bills on the navigation bar.

2. Click Setup Bills & Deposits on the Bills & Deposits bar.

3. Click the New button.

4. Click the Bill option button, and click Next.

5. Specify whether the bill is a recurring transaction or a one-time payment. If you specify that the payment occurs more than once, select a payment frequency in the Frequency field. Click Next.

6. Select Automatic Payment (Apay) from the Payment Method field and click Next.

7. Select the name of the account from which you want the payments to be made. The account must be set up with the Online Bill Payment service.

8. Enter the date you want the first payment to be made.

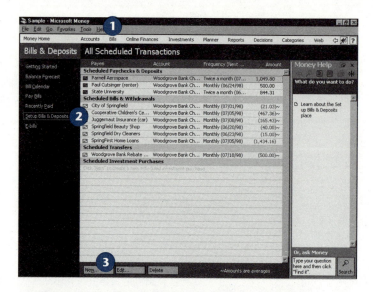

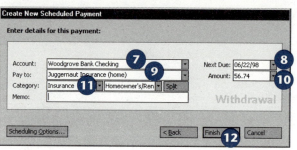

TIP

Be careful with automatic payments, because once you set them up, the payments are made whether or not you connect to the online services.

TIP

If you are creating a monthly automatic payment, the payment will be delivered on the same day of each month.

TIP

One month before an automatic payment is due, it will be downloaded to your account register as a reminder that it's coming up. Once it has been downloaded, you can make any changes you want (including canceling the payment).

9 Enter the name of the person or business you're paying.

10 Enter the payment amount.

11 Categorize the payment.

12 Click Finish.

13 Enter the number of payments or the date of the final payment. If you want payments to be made until you cancel them, leave both fields empty.

14 Click OK. If this is a new payee, fill in the boxes of the Online Payee Details dialog box and click OK.

15 Click Online Finances on the navigation bar.

16 Select the account for which you're setting up the automatic payment and click Go To.

17 Click Connect on the Online bar, and review the Automatic Payment information.

18 Click the Connect button to send the instructions.

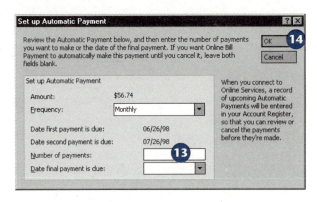

Set up Automatic Payment

Review the Automatic Payment below, and then enter the number of payments you want to make or the date of the final payment. If you want Online Bill Payment to automatically make this payment until you cancel it, leave both fields blank.

OK **14**
Cancel

Set up Automatic Payment

Amount:	$56.74
Frequency:	Monthly

Date first payment is due: 06/26/98

Date second payment is due: 07/26/98

Number of payments: **13**

Date final payment is due:

When you connect to Online Services, a record of upcoming Automatic Payments will be entered in your Account Register, so that you can review or cancel the payments before they're made.

10

Canceling Automatic Payments

You have two options for canceling an automatic payment. You can cancel an individual occurrence of the payment but keep the automatic payment in your payment calendar for the future, or you can delete all occurrences of the payment.

TIP

Money adds upcoming automatic payments to the register only if you connect to your bank within one month of the payment's due date.

TIP

You can also delete an individual automatic payment from within the Bills area by right-clicking the automatic payment and choosing the shortcut menu's Skip command. Then connect to your bank to send the cancellation instruction.

Cancel an Individual Automatic Payment

1 In the online account's register, right-click the transaction you want to cancel.

2 Choose the shortcut menu's Mark As command, and then choose the Mark As submenu's Void command.

3 Click Online Finances on the navigation bar.

4 Select the online account with the automatic payment cancellation instruction and click Go To.

5 Click Connect on the Online bar, and review the cancel payment instructions.

6 Click the Connect button to send the instruction.

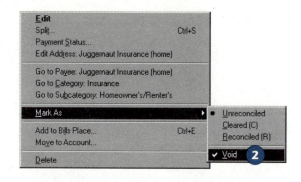

Permanently Cancel an Automatic Payment

1 Click Bills on the navigation bar.

2 Click Setup Bills & Deposits on the Bills & Deposits bar.

3 Select the automatic payment you want to cancel, and click Delete.

4 Click Yes to confirm the delete.

5 Click Online Finances on the navigation bar.

6 Select the account from which the automatic payment is made and click Go To.

7 Click Connect on the Online bar, and review the instructions to cancel the automatic payment.

8 Click the Connect button.

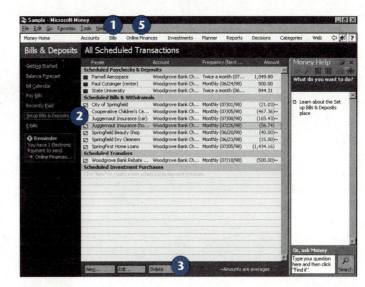

10

Transferring Money Online

As long as you have two accounts at the same bank and both are registered for the Online Banking Service, you can electronically transfer money between them.

TIP

For electronic transfers, you must use today's date. The transfer takes place at the end of the day. If you request an electronic transfer after the cut-off time, it is processed at the end of the following business day. Transfers to and from credit card accounts have an additional one-day delay.

TRY THIS

Check your statement on the day following the transfer to make sure the money was transferred.

Transfer Money Between Accounts

1. Display the register for the online account from which you want to transfer money.

2. Click the Transfer tab.

3. Click the down arrow in the Number field, and select Electronic Transfer (Xfer) from the list.

4. Click the down arrow in the From field, and select the name of the account from which you're transferring the money.

5. Enter the transfer date.

6. Click the down arrow in the To field, and select the name of the account to which you're transferring money.

7. Enter the amount you want transferred between the accounts.

8. Click Enter.

9. Connect to your bank to send the transfer instruction.

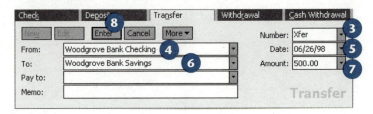

Sending E-Mail to Your Bank

You can send electronic mail to your bank to inquire about a payment, request a copy of a check, order new paper checks, or send a general purpose letter.

Write Letter...

TRY THIS

Click Contact Information on the Online bar to see your bank's contact information.

TIP

To delete a letter you have written, right-click the letter from the list of transactions to send and choose the shortcut menu's Remove command.

Send an E-Mail Message to Your Bank

1. Click Online Finances on the navigation bar.

2. Select the account concerning which you want to send a message and click Go To.

3. Click the Connect tab.

4. Click the Write Letter button.

5. Select the option that corresponds with the type of letter you want to send, and click Continue.

6. Write the letter.

7. Click OK.

8. Click Connect to send the letter.

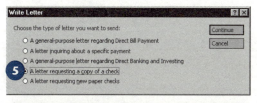

10

Researching Personal Finance Topics on the Internet

The Internet is the richest source of all types of personal financial information. Unfortunately, it's also the most disorganized. There isn't a single place to go to get all the information you want. You can get personal finance information from newsgroups, from mailing list messages, and on World Wide Web sites.

I'm not going to describe how to use all these features here because the procedure differs depending on your Internet service provider, on the Web browser you use, and on your e-mail client software. For purposes of this discussion, therefore, I assume you already have access to the Internet. So in this section, I'll tell you specifically where to locate personal finance information.

Newsgroups

An Internet *newsgroup* is really just an electronic bulletin board. Some people post messages on the bulletin board, and other people read them. A handful of newsgroups post messages on personal financial topics. As long as you have a newsgroup reader (such as Outlook Express, which comes as a part of Internet Explorer on the Money 99 CD) and access to the Internet or to an online service that hosts newsgroups, you can read the posted messages and even post your own.

At the time I am writing this, the following public newsgroups are available and active.

NEWSGROUP NAME	WHAT IT COVERS
aus.invest	Investments in Australia or of special interest to Australians
microsoft.public.investor	All types of investment discussion
microsoft.public.money	Tips and troubleshooting advice by Microsoft Money users
misc.invest	All types of investment discussion
misc.invest.canada	Investments in Canada or of special interest to Canadians
misc.invest.funds	Mutual fund investing
misc.invest.real-estate	Real estate investing
misc.invest.stocks	Common stock investments
misc.invest.stocks.penny	Penny stocks
misc.invest.technical	Technical analysis (charting) of securities
soc.college.financial-aid	Help finding and applying for financial aid
uk.finance	General finance information especially targeted for residents of the United Kingdom

Mailing Lists

Internet *mailing lists* are simply lists of electronic mail addresses. When someone mails a message to the mailing list, everyone whose name is on the list gets the message. This might seem like much ado about nothing, but because mailing lists cater to the interests of their members, mailing lists are powerful communication tools. Several Internet mailing lists provide useful personal information.

You can get a list of mailing lists organized by subject or by name by visiting the Web site at *www.neosoft.com/internet/paml/*. This Web site also lists the instructions for subscribing to each of the mailing lists. A few lists you might want to check out include: AAM-Talk, Financial Freedom Issues, InvestorGuide Weekly, investors-digest, Money Sense, persfin-digest, Timely Investment Information, Ultimate Credit Online Newsletter, and WALLSTREET.

World Wide Web Sites

The Internet provides hundreds of popular World Wide Web sites related to personal finance, including the online versions of several popular financial newspapers and magazines. Some sites are free; others require you to subscribe. One site you might be interested in is that of the Wall Street Journal, at *www.wsj.com*.

Another way to find Web sites related to the personal finance topic you're interested in is by using a search service such as Yahoo! at *www.yahoo.com*. You can use the search service of your choice to enter a personal finance word or phrase and build a list of Web sites falling under that category or including the text you entered.

Your Online Service Provider

In a general sense, online services such as America Online, CompuServe, Prodigy, and The Microsoft Network work the same way. Each provides up-to-the-minute news and delayed stock prices, special online columns and newsletters that cover personal financial topics, and personal financial chat rooms and bulletin boards where you can ask questions about investing. Most of the services also let you connect to online brokerage services.

Compared with haphazardly searching the Web, these online services provide a unique advantage. Usually, you can simply click a button, and the service displays a list of the personal financial or investing features it provides. The service often also lets you designate or customize your start page to list your investments.

10

Using Microsoft Investor

The Microsoft Investor Web site includes a wealth of up-to-the-minute investment and financial information, including late-breaking news and market information. It also includes several advanced investment features, such as online trading, portfolio tracking, and in-depth histories and reports to help you locate investments and make informed decisions when deciding on investment opportunities.

> **TIP**
>
> *Click Subscription Services to sign up for a free six-month subscription to Microsoft Investor. A subscription to Investor allows you to access more areas of the Web site, including Investment Finder.*

Navigate Microsoft Investor

1 Click Investments on the navigation bar.

2 Click Microsoft Investor on the Investments bar.

3 Click a topic hyperlink to go to that area on the Microsoft Investor Web site.

4 Use the new toolbar buttons to move through Microsoft Investor.

   ◆ Click Back to visit the page you previously visited.

   ◆ Click Forward to visit the page you last visited before clicking Back.

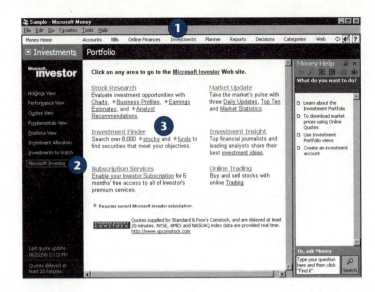

◆ Click Stop to stop downloading a page, for instance, if your computer stalls.

◆ Click Refresh to re-download the current page, for instance, if you needed to click Stop before it had completely down-loaded.

◆ Click Full Browser to increase the size of the browser window so that it fills your screen.

◆ Click Disconnect to disconnect from the Internet.

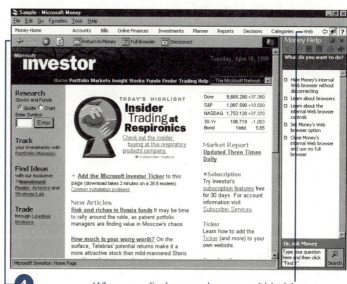

When you display your browser within Money, Money adds the Web item to the navigation bar. If you visit another area of Money, click Web to return to what you were last viewing on the Web.

10

The Money Home Page

The Money Home Page is a great way to quickly access technical support with Money and get the latest product information and tips for Money users. From the Money Home Page, you can also link to a wealth of personal finance resources and even send Microsoft Corporation any comments or suggestions you have for improving the program.

TIP

You can also access the Money Home Page without opening Money. Just connect to the Internet, open your Web browser, and then enter the address www.microsoft.com/ Money/.

TIP

Your screen will look a little different from the figure on this page because Microsoft constantly updates the Money Home Page.

Access the Money Home Page

1 Choose the Help menu's Microsoft On The Web command and the Microsoft On The Web submenu's Microsoft Money Home Page command.

2 Click one of the hyperlinks to access the information you're looking for.

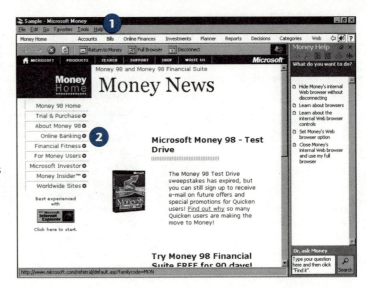

Managing a Small Business with Money

Although Microsoft Money is chiefly a personal finance program, it is also perfectly suited for keeping financial records for many small businesses. Before you start using Money for small business accounting, however, you need to think about whether Money will work for you. Here's a breakdown of what Money can and cannot do. Use this list to determine whether Money will meet your needs or if you should instead upgrade to a complete small business accounting program.

Tasks you can complete with Money:

◆ Print checks for a business

◆ Track business bank accounts and business investments

◆ Prepare payroll for salaried employees

Tasks beyond the scope of Money:

◆ Print business forms such as invoices

◆ Track inventory, accounts payable accounts, and loans payable accounts

◆ Calculate payroll expenses, depreciation, and bid amounts

◆ Track owner's equity

Adding Business Income and Expense Categories

Before you can start keeping your books with Money, you need to set up the bank account in which you'll make business transactions. Then you need to create categories to track your business income and expenses. Although you can create your own categories, you will want to use the categories that are on the Schedule C business tax return.

> ## TIP
> *If you're using the same category list to track business and personal expenses, you may want to start each category name with the word Business or the abbreviation Bus to identify it as a business category.*

Add an Income or Expense Category

1. Click Categories on the navigation bar.

2. Click the New button.

3. Click the Create A New Category option button, and click Next.

4. Enter a name for the business income or expense category.

5. Specify whether the new category is an income or an expense category by selecting the appropriate option, and then click Next.

6. Indicate that an income category falls into the Other Income group, or indicate that an expense category falls into the Other Expense group.

7. Click Finish.

8. Repeat steps 2 through 7 to add all the business income and business expense categories you need.

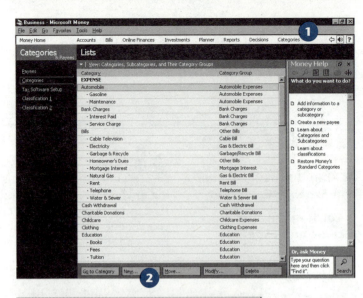

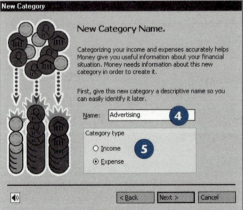

Identifying the Tax Treatment of a Category

After you add an income or expense category, you need to describe how Money should treat the category for income tax purposes. Specifically, you need to identify where the category is reported for income tax purposes.

TIP

If you don't know which form you'll use at the end of the year—Schedule C or Schedule C-EZ—specify the Schedule C-EZ form.

TIP

If you will use Money to keep track of more than one business's books, each business needs to use its own set of categories.

Describe the Tax Treatment of a Category

1. Click Categories on the navigation bar.

2. Click the Tax Software Setup tab in the Categories bar.

3. Click the category you want to describe.

4. Check the Include On Tax Reports box.

5. Use the Tax Form box to specify the tax form on which this category should be reported.

6. Use the Form Line box to specify the line of the tax form specified in step 5 on which this category should be reported.

7. To keep the books for more than one sole proprietorship, use the Form Copy box to identify each sole proprietorship and Schedule C or C-EZ combination: 1 for the first one, 2 for the second one, and so on.

8. Repeat steps 3 through 7 for each of the business categories you will work with.

Recording Business Income and Expenses

Once you set up the accounts and categories you need for tracking business income and expenses, you're ready to begin recording the income and expenses.

Business Checking

SEE ALSO

For more information about creating an account, see "Setting Up Bank Accounts" on page 16.

Record Business Income

1 Display the business account's register.

2 Click the Deposit tab, and if necessary, click New.

3 Enter the invoice number if applicable.

4 Enter the deposit date.

5 Enter the customer's name, or select the name from the From field.

6 Enter the amount of the deposit.

7 Click the down arrow in the Category field, and select the category that describes the deposit's income category.

8 Optionally, enter a description of the deposit.

9 Click Enter.

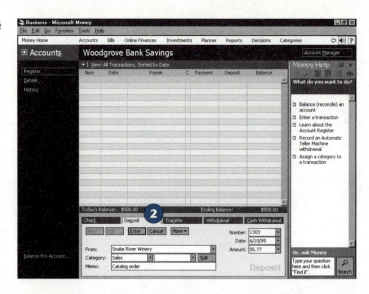

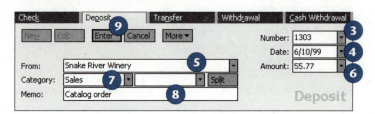

SEE ALSO

For a list of data-entry tricks you can use to speed the process of entering transactions into an account register, see "Timesaving Tips for Entering Transactions" on page 27.

Record a Business Expense

1 Display the business account's register.

2 Click the Check tab, and if necessary, click New.

3 Enter the check number.

4 Enter the check date.

5 Enter the name of the person or business you're paying, or select it from the Pay To field.

6 Enter the amount of the check.

7 Click the down arrow in the Category field, and select the category that describes the check's expense category.

8 Optionally, enter a description of the check.

9 Click Enter.

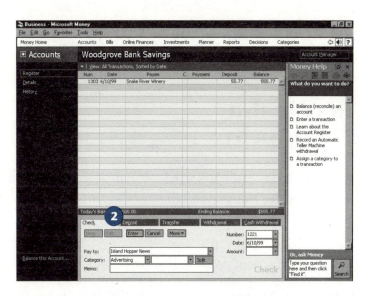

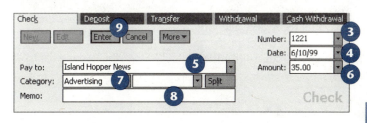

11

Preparing for Accounts Receivable Accounting

Although Money isn't really set up to invoice customers and to track the amounts that you've billed to and collected from customers, with a little coercion, you can use Money to keep track of invoices and payments. You just need to set up an accounts receivable account and then use a word processing program to produce the actual invoice.

Accounts Receivable

Set Up an Accounts Receivable Account

1 Click Accounts on the navigation bar once or twice to display the Account Manager window.

2 Click the New Account button.

3 Leave the Held At field empty, and click Next.

4 Select Asset from the list, and click Next.

5 Enter a name for the account so that you can recognize it as your accounts receivable account. You could name it simply "Accounts Receivable," for example. Click Next.

6 Enter zero in the What Is The Value Of This Asset field.

7 Click Next.

8 When Money asks if you want to associate a loan account with the asset, select the No option and click Finish.

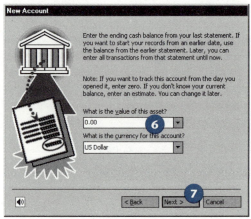

Cash-Basis vs. Accrual-Basis Accounting

Cash-basis accounting counts any checking account deposit as income and any checking account withdrawal as an expense. Cash-basis accounting is commonly employed in small businesses because it's easy to use. But it's usually less accurate than the alternative, accrual-basis accounting, in the way that it measures profits. Accrual-basis accounting counts income when you bill customers and counts expense when you charge or incur bills. The problem with accrual-basis accounting, however, is that to use it, you need to understand double-entry bookkeeping.

Cash-basis accounting counts income when you receive the cash and counts expense when you pay a bill. This might sound correct, but it tends to produce some funny profit measurements. For example, if you're using cash-basis accounting to measure your profits, your profits increase when you delay payment of your bills. And if you're using cash-basis accounting and a customer's check arrives next month instead of this month, your profits for the current month decrease. For example, you can easily increase or decrease your records of profits for the year by simply waiting until January 1 to write a check for something purchased during December or to enter a deposit for a service rendered during December. Accrual-basis accounting counts income when you bill the customer and counts expense when you charge some amount or incur some expense. Accrual-basis accounting more accurately measures your profits in a given time period, but it's more complicated and more work because you use double-entry bookkeeping. All large companies and most small companies use accrual-basis accounting because it is less susceptible to manipulation and is employed by all auditors and certified public accountants.

11

Recording an Invoice

How you record an invoice depends on the accounting system you use. If you want to use cash-basis accounting, you simply use your accounts receivable account to list your unpaid invoices. If you use accrual-basis accounting, you record an invoice as an increase in the accounts receivable account, and then you record the payment as a transfer from the accounts receivable account to the bank account.

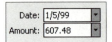

Record an Invoice with Cash-Basis Accounting

1. Display the accounts receivable account.

2. Click the Increase tab, and if necessary, click New.

3. Enter the invoice date.

4. Enter the name of the customer.

5. Enter the invoice amount.

6. Leave the Category fields empty.

7. Optionally, enter a description of the invoice; for example, a purchase order number.

8. Click Enter.

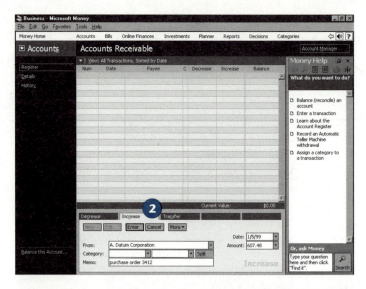

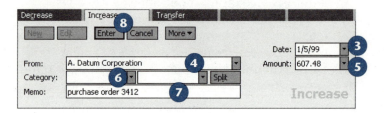

TIP

If your accounting system is sophisticated enough that you require an accounts payable account to track bills as you incur them, you should consider upgrading to a small business accounting program.

SEE ALSO

For more information about setting up business income and expense categories, see "Adding Business Income and Expense Categories" on page 172.

Record an Invoice with Accrual-Basis Accounting

1 Display the accounts receivable account.

2 Click the Increase tab, and if necessary, click New.

3 Enter the invoice date.

4 Enter the name of the customer.

5 Enter the invoice amount.

6 Use the Category fields to specify an income category. By doing this, you count a customer invoice as income when you bill rather than when you collect.

7 Optionally, enter a description of the invoice; for example, a purchase order number.

8 Click Enter.

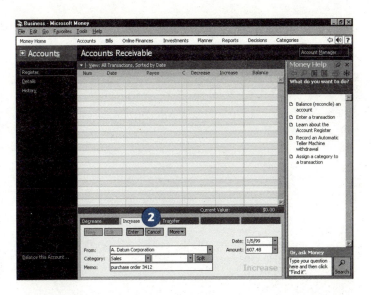

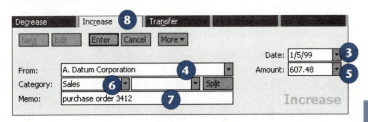

Recording a Customer Payment

How you record a customer payment depends on the accounting system you use. To record a customer payment using cash-basis accounting, you first record the customer's check as a deposit in the bank account, and then you record the decrease in the accounts receivable account. To record a customer payment using accrual-basis accounting, you record a deposit in the bank account and transfer the money from the accounts receivable account.

To:	Woodgrove Bank Checking
From:	Accounts Receivable
Pay to:	A. Datum Corporation
Memo:	purchase order 3412

TIP

Don't forget to record and categorize the customer's check in the business account's register. For more information on how to do this, see page 174.

Record a Customer Payment with Cash-Basis Accounting

1. Display the accounts receivable account's register.

2. Click the Decrease tab, and if necessary, click New.

3. Enter the payment date.

4. Select the customer's name from the Pay To field.

5. Enter the amount of the check.

6. Leave the Category fields empty.

7. Optionally, enter a description of the check, such as the customer's check number, in the Memo field.

8. Click Enter.

9. Mark the invoice(s) that the customer's check pays and the customer's check as reconciled by right-clicking each transaction and choosing the shortcut menu's Mark As command and the Mark As submenu's Reconciled command.

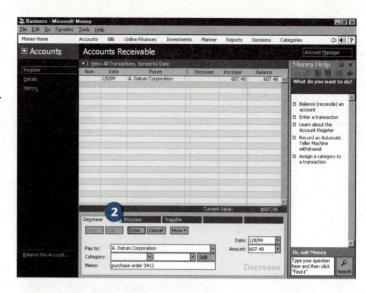

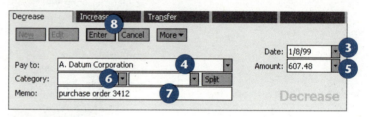

Record a Customer Payment with Accrual-Basis Accounting

1 Display the business's bank account register.

2 Click the Deposit tab, and if necessary, click New.

3 Enter the customer's check number.

4 Enter the payment date.

5 Click the down arrow in the From field, and select the name of the customer making the payment.

6 Enter the amount of the check.

7 Enter Transfer in the Category field.

8 Click the down arrow in the Subcategory field, and select the name of the accounts receivable account.

9 Optionally, enter a description of the check in the Memo field.

10 Click Enter.

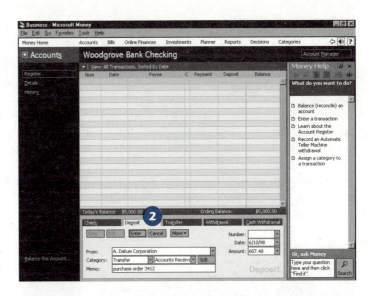

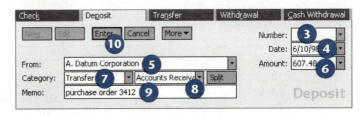

11

Monitoring Accounts Receivable

On a regular basis, you need to review your accounts receivable. In particular, you want to watch out for delinquent customer invoices—invoices that should have been paid but haven't been paid. To do this, you can produce a report that summarizes the transactions in the accounts receivable account and sorts the information by customer name.

Produce an Accounts Receivable Report

1. Click Reports on the navigation bar.

2. Click Spending Habits on the Reports & Charts bar.

3. Select Account Transactions from the list.

4. Click the Go To Report/ Chart button.

5. Click Customize on the Accounts bar to open the Customize Report dialog box.

6. Click the Layout tab.

7. Specify which pieces of register information you want to appear on the report. If you aren't using the Category fields when you enter transactions, you can clear the Category box, for instance. If you are using the Memo field to store information such as invoice numbers or check numbers, you should make sure the Memo box is checked.

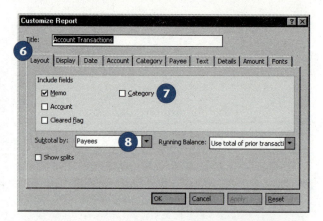

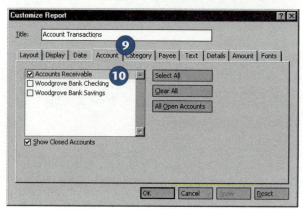

8 Select Payees from the Subtotal By field.

9 Click the Account tab.

10 Select your accounts receivable account.

11 Click the Details tab.

12 Select Unreconciled Transactions from the Status field.

13 Click OK.

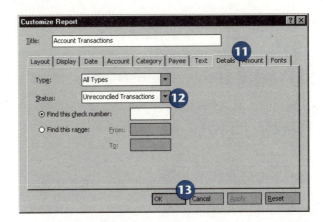

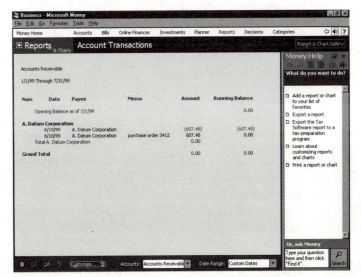

Setting Up Payroll Accounts to Track Withholdings

Money doesn't provide a payroll feature as such, but it can dramatically reduce the work of preparing a payroll. You can use Money, for example, to record and print payroll checks. You can also produce quarterly and yearly payroll reports that you can use to prepare payroll tax returns. The first thing you need to do to begin tracking payroll expenses using Money is to set up payroll liability accounts. Specifically, you need liability accounts to track Social Security taxes, Medicare taxes, and federal income tax withholdings.

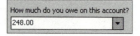

Set Up Payroll Liability Accounts

1. Click Accounts on the navigation bar once or twice to display the Account Manager window.

2. Click the New Account button to start the New Account Wizard.

3. Leave the Held At field empty, and click Next.

4. Select Liability from the list of account types, and click Next.

5. Enter a name for the liability account. For example, use the names Social Security, Medicare, and Federal Tax to track the different taxes you withhold and owe. Click Next.

6. Enter the amount you currently owe for the tax, and click Finish.

7. Repeat steps 2 through 6 to set up a separate account for each of the taxes.

Payroll Tax Reporting Requirements

To meet the federal payroll tax and reporting requirements, your first step is to get an employer tax identification number. This number is equivalent to your personal Social Security number—it identifies you as an employer and is used by the government to track transactions relating specifically to your responsibilities as an employer. To get an employer tax identification number, contact the Internal Revenue Service and ask for an SS-4 form. This form, which is very simple to fill out, tells the IRS you want to hire an employee.

Once you request an employer tax identification number, the IRS knows you're an employer and sends you the federal tax deposit coupons you use to remit the money withheld from employees' paychecks. And, at the end of the quarter and the end of the year, the IRS sends you the payroll tax returns you need to complete: the end-of-quarter 941 return to report the wages you've paid for the quarter and the end-of-year 940 return to report any federal unemployment tax you owe.

The IRS also sends you a copy of the *Employer's Tax Guide*. This booklet, which is sometimes called a "Circular E," tells you how much federal income tax, Social Security tax, and Medicare tax you're supposed to withhold from an employee's paycheck. You need this booklet to prepare payroll checks. Watch for it, and don't lose it.

State and Local Payroll Tax and Reporting Requirements

Your state also has payroll tax and reporting requirements that you need to meet. States, for example, require employers to pay unemployment insurance and disability insurance, also known as *workman's compensation*. Most states have a state income tax that you, as an employer, need to withhold from employee checks and then remit to the state. You may also have local county or city payroll tax reporting requirements.

I can't give you precise instructions for meeting state and local payroll tax reporting requirements because they vary from state to state. Contact the state or local employment tax office, and tell them you are hiring an employee or several employees. The office will put you on its list of employers. Typically, as soon as this happens, you get instructions on what you're supposed to do. And you periodically get payroll tax returns you're supposed to fill out and return. (End-of-quarter payroll tax returns are common, for example.)

Other Employee Reporting Requirements

In addition to the payroll tax and reporting requirements described in the preceding paragraphs, employers are also required to perform other tasks. The Immigration and Naturalization Service, for example, requires employers to verify that their employees are U.S. citizens, Permanent Residents, or have a work visa. Some states have special reporting requirements, for example, to help track down parents who aren't making court-ordered child support payments. And there are often other special reporting requirements as well.

11

Setting Up Payroll Categories

Once you've set up your payroll liability accounts, you need to set up several new payroll expense categories. Specifically, you need to set up a category called Payroll and several subcategories within this category to track your taxes and payroll expenses.

TIP

Tax-related categories appear in the Tax Software Setup window with an X in the Tax field. Make sure that all tax-related categories have a tax form and line assigned to them in the Tax Form and Line fields. For more information on assigning categories a line on a particular tax form, see page 173.

Set Up the Payroll Expense Category

1. Click Categories on the navigation bar.

2. Click the New button.

3. Click the Create a New Category option button, and click Next.

4. Enter the new category name as Payroll in the Name field.

5. Click the Expense option button, and click Next.

6. Select Other Expense from the list.

7. Click Finish.

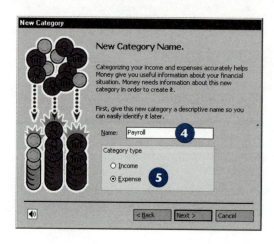

New Category Name.

Categorizing your income and expenses accurately helps Money give you useful information about your financial situation. Money needs information about this new category in order to create it.

First, give this new category a descriptive name so you can easily identify it later.

Name: Payroll

Category type
○ Income
● Expense

< Back   Next >   Cancel

Set Up Payroll Expense Subcategories

1. Click Categories on the navigation bar.

2. Select Payroll from the Categories field.

3. Click New.

4. Click the Add A Subcategory To Payroll option button, and click Next.

5. Enter a name for the new category in the Name field. For example, use the name Gross Wages to track gross wages.

6. Click Next and Finish.

7. Repeat steps 3 through 6 to add the other payroll subcategories.

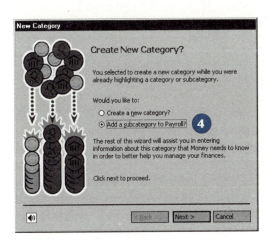

New Category

Create New Category?

You selected to create a new category while you were already highlighting a category or subcategory.

Would you like to:

○ Create a new category?

⊙ Add a subcategory to Payroll?   **4**

The rest of this wizard will assist you in entering information about this category that Money needs to know in order to better help you manage your finances.

Click next to proceed.

[< Back] [Next >] [Cancel]

Writing Payroll Checks

Once you've set up the payroll accounts and payroll categories you need, preparing a payroll check is a snap. You just need to figure out how much you're supposed to withhold for the employee based on the information the employee provided on his or her W-4 form and the tables listed in the current *Employer's Tax Guide*. Then you enter the amounts you calculate in the Split Transaction dialog box.

TIP

The payroll preparation instructions provided here not only work for business employees. They work for household employees—such as childcare workers—too.

Record a Check to an Employee

1 Display the business bank account's register, click the Check tab, and if necessary, click New.

2 Enter the check number, date, and pay to information in the usual way.

3 Click the Split button.

4 Describe the gross wages on the first line of the Split Transaction dialog box by specifying the Category as Payroll and the Subcategory as Gross Wages. Enter the gross wages in the Amount field.

5 Describe the federal income taxes withheld from the paycheck on the second line by specifying the Category as Transfer and the Subcategory as Federal Tax. Enter the amount in the Amount field.

6 Describe the Social Security taxes paid by the employee through withholding on the third line by specifying the Category as Transfer and the Subcategory as Social Security. Enter the amount in the Amount field.

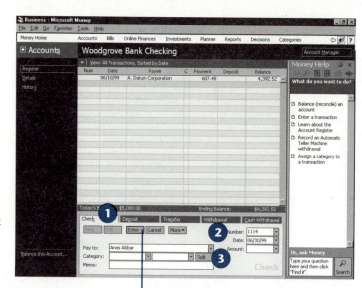

Click Enter to enter the payroll check into the register.

TIP

Both the employer and employee pay a Medicare tax equal to 1.45% of the employee's gross wages. The employer and employees both also typically pay a Social Security tax equal to 6.2% of the employee's gross wages.

TIP

To record the check you use to pay the Internal Revenue Service for some payroll tax you owe, you just write the check for whatever amount you owe. Then you record the check as a transfer to the liability account.

7 Describe the Medicare taxes paid by the employee through withholding on the fourth line by specifying the Category as Transfer and the Subcategory as Medicare. Enter the amount in the Amount field.

8 Enter the employer's matching Social Security expense on the fifth line by specifying the Category as Payroll and the Subcategory as Employer's Social Security.

9 Enter the amount of money owed the federal government for Social Security tax on the sixth line by specifying the Category as Transfer and the Subcategory as Social Security.

10 Enter the employer's matching Medicare taxes on the seventh line by specifying the Category as Payroll and the Subcategory as Employer's Medicare.

11 Enter the amount of money owed the federal government for this Medicare tax on the eighth line by specifying the Category as Transfer and the Subcategory as Medicare.

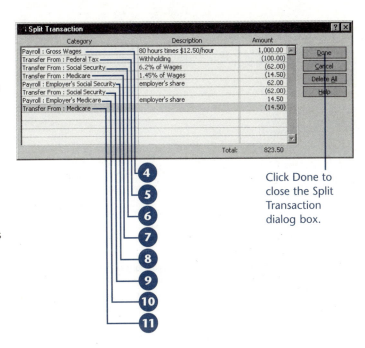

Click Done to close the Split Transaction dialog box.

11

Preparing W-2 and W-3 Forms

The other payroll task you must complete is the annual preparation of W-2 forms and the W-3 form. You complete a W-2 for each employee to summarize the gross pay earned over the year and the taxes withheld over the year. The W-3 summarizes all the W-2s. Although Money won't print these forms for you, you can use it to calculate the needed information and display it in a report.

Produce a Payroll Transaction Report

1. Click Reports on the navigation bar.

2. Click Spending Habits on the Reports & Charts bar.

3. Double-click the Who Is Getting My Money selection in the Spending Habits list.

4. Click Customize to open the Customize Report dialog box.

5. Change the report's title by clicking the Title field and typing *Employee Wages Summary*.

6. Click the Layout tab.

7. Click the down arrow in the Rows field, and select Subcategories from the list.

8. Click the down arrow in the Columns field, and select Payees from the list.

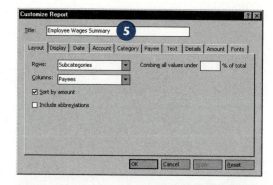

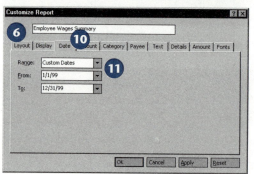

SEE ALSO

For more information on printing reports, see "Printing Reports" on pages 64–65.

TIP

If Money initially displays a chart instead of a report, click the Report button. The Report button shows a report icon and appears in the lower-left corner of the window.

TIP

You should also be able to use the Employee Wages Summary report to prepare the quarterly and annual payroll tax returns.

9 Enter *0* into the Combine All Values Under X % Of Total field.

10 Click the Date tab.

11 Use the Range options to tell Money for which year you want to prepare the W-2s and W-3.

12 Click the Category tab.

13 Click the Clear All button.

14 Select the Payroll expense category and the Payroll subcategories from the list, and click OK.

15 Click OK to produce the Employee Wages Summary report.

16 Print the report by choosing the File menu's Print command. With the help of the Internal Revenue Service instructions, you should be able to use the information provided by your printed report to complete the W-2 and W-3 forms.

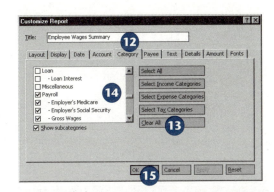

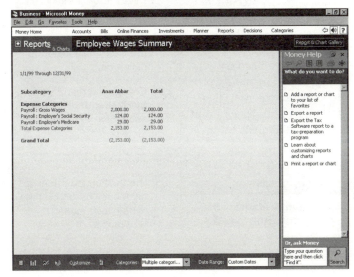

Measuring Profits

There are many reasons for owning or operating a small business. Autonomy, for one, or maybe just plain fun. But for a business to survive, the business must produce profits. Accordingly, on a regular basis, you need to calculate whether you're making a profit. As long as you've been collecting information about your income and expenses, it is very easy to produce a Profit and Loss Statement using Money.

TIP

Getting information on your competitors' profits. *Both Robert Morris & Associates and Standard and Poor's publish financial statistics on a variety of businesses. The data is arranged by size of business and by standard industry classification, or SIC, codes. You can obtain these publications at your local library.*

Produce a Profit and Loss Statement

1 Click Reports on the navigation bar.

2 Click Spending Habits on the Reports & Charts bar.

3 Select Income vs. Spending from the Spending Habits list.

4 Click the Go To Report/ Chart button.

5 Click Customize to open the Customize Report dialog box.

6 Change the report's title by clicking the Title field and typing *Profit and Loss Statement*.

7 Click the Date tab.

8 Use the Range options to tell Money for which time period you want to measure profits.

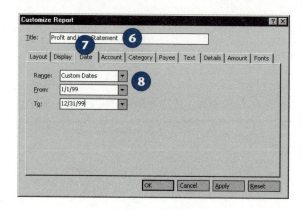

TIP

The Dates field provides several common profit reporting periods. As a general rule, you want to measure profits on a monthly and an annual basis.

SEE ALSO

For more information about creating and customizing charts, see "Working with Reports" on page 56.

9 Click the Category tab.

10 Select the business income and expense categories that you want to appear on your Profit and Loss Statement from the list.

11 Click OK to produce the Profit and Loss Statement.

12 Print the statement by choosing the File menu's Print command.

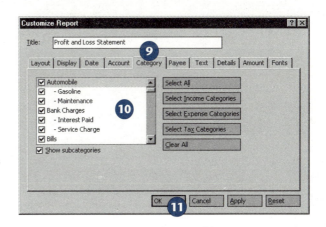

Measuring Cash Flow

Over the long haul, a business can't survive without profits, but cash flow is more important in the short run. To make it through the next month or quarter, for example, you need to have enough cash to pay all your bills and to make any needed investments in new machinery or equipment.

Produce a Monthly Cash Flow Statement

1 Click Reports on the navigation bar.

2 Click Spending Habits on the Reports & Charts bar.

3 Select Monthly Cash Flow from the Spending Habits list.

4 Click the Go To Report/ Chart button.

5 Click Customize to open the Customize Report dialog box.

6 Click the Date tab.

7 Use the Range options to tell Money for which time period you want to measure cash flow.

8 Click the Account tab.

9 Click the Select All button to make sure that transfers to and from all your accounts are included.

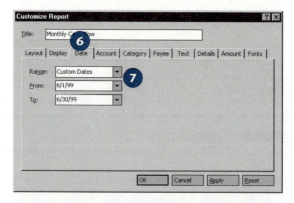

Why does my cash flow differ from my profit?

If you record your business income when you deposit customer payments and you record your business expenses when you write checks, you use cash-basis accounting. In this case, your profit and loss statement will closely resemble your cash-flow statement. The only differences will result from account transfers to and from your bank accounts. These transfers appear on cash flow statements because they involve cash moving in or out of a bank account. But they don't appear on profit and loss statements.

10 Click the Category tab.

11 Select the business income and expense categories that you want to appear on your Cash Flow Statement from the list.

12 Click OK to produce the Cash Flow Statement.

13 Print the statement by choosing the File menu's Print command.

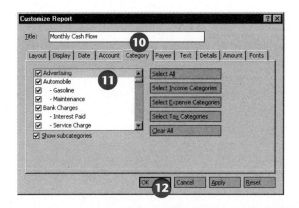

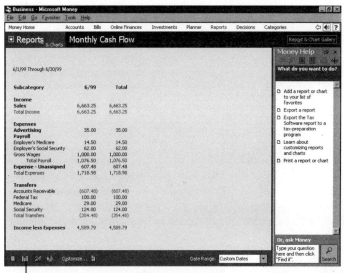

To view your Cash Flow Statement in a bar chart, click the Bar Chart icon.

11

Measuring Net Worth

With a balance sheet, you tally your assets and liabilities and calculate the difference between these two amounts to get your business's net worth. A balance sheet provides several pieces of useful information. It lets you assess the liquidity of your business, helps you calculate return on investment figures, and provides information you need to determine how fast you can grow your business.

Produce a Balance Sheet

1 Click Reports on the navigation bar.

2 Click What I Have on the Reports & Charts bar.

3 Select Account Balances from the What I Have list.

4 Click the Go To Report/ Chart button.

5 Click the Customize button to open the Customize Report dialog box.

6 Change the report's title by clicking in the Title field and typing *Balance Sheet*.

7 Click the Layout tab.

8 Use the Show Balances As Of field to specify the date for which you want the account balance calculated.

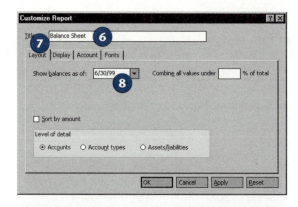

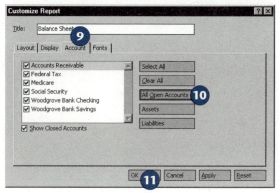

How fast can I grow my business? *In general, you can grow your business only as fast as you can grow your net worth. For example, if you want to grow your business by 25 percent annually, you need to grow your net worth by 25 percent annually. Because a small business usually increases its net worth only by reinvesting profits, however, these reinvested profits limit your growth. For example, if reinvested profits as a percentage of net worth equal 20 percent, you can only grow your business by 20 percent.*

Interpreting the Balance Sheet. *A general rule of thumb is that the sum of your cash, accounts receivable, and any investments should at least be equal to your short-term debts. Your short-term debts include liabilities you have to pay in the coming year, any amounts you now owe employees or creditors, business credit-card balances, and the loan principal payments you'll make over the next year. You should be able to get all this information from your Balance Sheet.*

9 Click the Account tab.

10 Click the All Open Accounts button.

11 Click OK to produce the Balance Sheet.

12 Print the Balance Sheet by choosing the File menu's Print command.

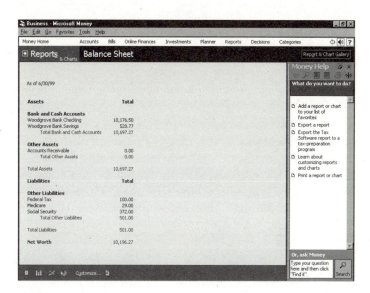

Preparing Income Tax Returns

If you use Money for your business bookkeeping, you want to be able to produce reports that summarize the required information for your federal and state income tax returns. If you're just starting a business, you'll first need to know which form you'll be using. The following table lists the standard federal income tax forms that businesses file.

FORM	USE IT TO REPORT
1040 Schedule C	Profit or loss from a sole proprietorship
1040 Schedule C-EZ	Profit or loss from a small sole proprietorship
1040 Schedule F	Income and expenses from farming
1040 Schedule SE	Tax due on income from self-employment
Form 1120	Income and expenses for a corporation
Form 1120A	Income and expenses for a corporation with gross receipts of less that $500,000
Form 1120S	Annual information for an S-corporation
Form 1065	Annual information for a partnership

You can download the most recent copies of these forms and schedules, along with the instructions that go with them, from the IRS Web site at *http://www.irs.ustreas.gov*.

The figure on the next page shows an example of Schedule C from Form 1040 for 1997. If you're a sole proprietor, you can use the income and expenses listed on this form as a basis for your categories in Money. If a more recent form is available when you set up your categories in Money, however, you should use it. Don't worry if the most recent form you can get is from the previous year. Forms aren't finalized until late in the year, and yet you need to track your income and expenses from the beginning of the year.

Part I   **Income**

1	Gross receipts or sales. **Caution:** *If this income was reported to you on Form W-2 and the "Statutory employee" box on that form was checked, see page C-2 and check here* . . . . ▶ ☐	**1**		
2	Returns and allowances	**2**		
3	Subtract line 2 from line 1	**3**		
4	Cost of goods sold (from line 42 on page 2)	**4**		
5	**Gross profit.** Subtract line 4 from line 3	**5**		
6	Other income, including Federal and state gasoline or fuel tax credit or refund (see page C-2) . . .	**6**		
7	**Gross income.** Add lines 5 and 6 . . . . ▶	**7**		

Part II   **Expenses.** Enter expenses for business use of your home **only** on line 30.

8	Advertising	**8**		19	Pension and profit-sharing plans	**19**	
9	Bad debts from sales or services (see page C-3) . .	**9**		20	Rent or lease (see page C-4):		
				a	Vehicles, machinery, and equipment .	**20a**	
10	Car and truck expenses (see page C-3)	**10**		b	Other business property . .	**20b**	
11	Commissions and fees . .	**11**		21	Repairs and maintenance . .	**21**	
12	Depletion	**12**		22	Supplies (not included in Part III) .	**22**	
13	Depreciation and section 179 expense deduction (not included in Part III) (see page C-3) . .	**13**		23	Taxes and licenses	**23**	
				24	Travel, meals, and entertainment:		
				a	Travel	**24a**	
14	Employee benefit programs (other than on line 19) . . .	**14**		b	Meals and entertainment .		
15	Insurance (other than health) .	**15**		c	Enter 50% of line 24b subject to limitations (see page C-4) .		
16	Interest:						
a	Mortgage (paid to banks, etc.) .	**16a**		d	Subtract line 24c from line 24b .	**24d**	
b	Other	**16b**		25	Utilities	**25**	
17	Legal and professional services	**17**		26	Wages (less employment credits) .	**26**	
18	Office expense	**18**		27	Other expenses (from line 48 on page 2)	**27**	

11

Index

ATM withdrawals, recording, 23
AutoComplete feature, 27
automatic payments
 canceling, 162–63
 creating, 160–61
automobiles. *See* cars
average annual return, 71

backup files, 8, 9, 13
balances. *See* account balances; statements, bank
balance sheets, 196–97
balancing bank statements, 38–41
bank accounts. *See also* accounts
 adding downloaded records to account register, 155
 closing, 42
 creating Money accounts for, 16
 downloading records, 154
 problems balancing, 40–41
 reconciling, 38–41
 recording service charges, 38
 storing information about, 18
 transferring funds online, 164
banks
 sending e-mail to, 165
 service charges, 38
 setting up Money accounts, 16
 setting up online services, 152–53
 transferring funds online, 164

basis, adjusted, 142
bill paying
 automatic payment, 160–63
 canceling electronic payments, 159
 checking status of electronic payments, 159
 entering electronic payments, 156–57
 recording transactions, 34
 recurring bills, 32
 sending electronic payments, 158
 setting up online services, 152–53
boats, tracking as assets, 101
bonds
 average annual return, 71
 recording accrued interest, 130
 recording discounts, 128–29
 recording holdings in Portfolio, 115
 recording interest, 127
 recording premiums, 128
 recording purchases, 120
 recording sales, 122
brokerage fees, recording, 125
Budget Planner, 80–81
budgets
 creating in Microsoft Money, 80–81
 tips for budgeting, 82–83
bunching tax deductions, 94–95
business accounts. *See also* small business
 accounts receivable, 176, 182–83
 adding categories, 172–73
 cash-basis *vs.* accrual-basis accounting, 177, 178–81

business accounts, *continued*
 recording customer payments, 180–81
 recording expenses, 175
 recording income, 174
 recording invoices, 178–79
 setting up, 172–73

calculators
 overview, 86–87
 quick calculations, 27
 Tuition Savings Calculator, 86–87
capital improvements, 142, 143
cars
 interest calculations, 103
 setting up loan account, 102–3
 tracking as assets, 101
cash accounts, 113
cash-basis accounting
 cash flow *vs.* profits, 195
 defined, 177
 recording customer payments, 180
 recording invoices, 178
cash flow statements, 194–95
casualty insurance, keeping asset lists for, 101
categories
 adding to list, 22
 assigning to checks, 22
 assigning to deposits, 19
 for business income and expenses, 172–73, 199
 deleting from list, 30
 IRS Schedule C, 199
 lists of, 30–31

categories, *continued*
 moving, 30
 for payroll expenses, 186–87
 for real estate investments, 140, 147
 renaming, 31
 splitting transactions, 29
 tax-related, 172–73, 186, 199
certificates of deposit, tracking, 113
charts
 adding to My Favorites list, 57
 creating, 56
 printing, 65
checkbook
 benefits of computerizing, 15
 Microsoft Money as, 15
 setting up Money account, 16
checking accounts
 deleting transactions, 34
 editing transactions, 34
 entering transactions, 19–23
 opening account register, 17
 printing checks, 24–25
 reconciling, 38–41
 recording ATM withdrawals, 23
 recording checks, 22
 recording deposits, 19
 recording expenses, 22–23
 recording paychecks, 20–21
 recording recurring transactions, 32–33
 recording transfers, 28
 setting up in Money, 16
 splitting transactions, 29
 tips for entering transactions, 27
check register. *See* account register
checks
 printing, 24–25
 splitting transactions, 29

The manuscript for this book was prepared and submitted to Microsoft Press in electronic form. Text files were prepared using Microsoft Word 97. Pages were composed by Stephen L. Nelson, Inc., using PageMaker for Windows, with text in Stone Sans and display type in Stone Serif and Stone Serif Semibold. Composed pages were delivered to the printer as electronic prepress files.

Cover Designer

Tim Girvin Design

Interior Graphic Designer

designLab
Kim Eggleston

Graphic Layout

Stefan Knorr

Indexer

Julie Kawabata

mspress.microsoft.com

 **Microsoft Press Online** is your road map to the best available print and multimedia materials—resources that will help you maximize the effectiveness of Microsoft® software products. Our goal is making it easy and convenient for you to find exactly the Microsoft Press® book or interactive product you need, as well as bringing you the latest in training and certification materials from Microsoft Press.

Where do you want to go today?® ***Microsoft*** Press

Microsoft Press has titles
to help everyone—
from new users
to seasoned developers—

Step by Step Series
Self-paced tutorials for classroom instruction or individualized study

Starts Here™ Series
Interactive instruction on CD-ROM that helps students learn by doing

Field Guide Series
Concise, task-oriented A–Z references for quick, easy answers—anywhere

Official Series
Timely books on a wide variety of Internet topics geared for advanced users

All User Training   All User Reference

Quick Course® Series
Fast, to-the-point instruction for new users

At a Glance Series
Quick visual guides for task-oriented instruction

Running Series
A comprehensive curriculum alternative to standard documentation books

start faster
and go farther!

The wide selection of books and CD-ROMs published by Microsoft Press contain something for every level of user and every area of interest, from just-in-time online training tools to development tools for professional programmers. Look for them at your bookstore or computer store today!

Professional Select Editions Series
Advanced titles geared for the system administrator or technical support career path

Microsoft® Certified Professional Training
The Microsoft Official Curriculum for certification exams

Best Practices Series
Candid accounts of the new movement in software development

Microsoft Programming Series
The foundations of software development

Professional   Developers

Microsoft Press® Interactive
Integrated multimedia courseware for all levels

Strategic Technology Series
Easy-to-read overviews for decision makers

Microsoft Professional Editions
Technical information straight from the source

Solution Developer Series
Comprehensive titles for intermediate to advanced developers

Microsoft Press

mspress.microsoft.com